BEST-EVER
SALAD RECIPES

BEST-EVER
SALAD RECIPES

DELICIOUS SEASONAL SALADS FOR ALL OCCASIONS: 180 SENSATIONAL
RECIPES SHOWN IN 245 FABULOUS PHOTOGRAPHS

Editor: Anne Hildyard

HERMES
HOUSE

This edition is published by Hermes House,
an imprint of Anness Publishing Ltd,
Blaby Road, Wigston, Leicestershire LE18 4SE;
info@anness.com

www.hermeshouse.com; www.annesspublishing.com

If you like the images in this book and would
like to investigate using them for publishing,
promotions or advertising, please visit our website
www.practicalpictures.com for more information.

Publisher: Joanna Lorenz
Editor: Anne Hildyard
Designer: Nigel Partridge
Proofreading Manager: Lindsay Zamponi
Production Controller: Wendy Lawson

ETHICAL TRADING POLICY

At Anness Publishing we believe that business
should be conducted in an ethical and ecologically
sustainable way, with respect for the environment
and a proper regard to the replacement of the
natural resources we employ.

As a publisher, we use a lot of wood pulp in
high-quality paper for printing, and that wood
commonly comes from spruce trees. We are
therefore currently growing more than 750,000
trees in three Scottish forest plantations:
Berrymoss (130 hectares/320 acres), West Touxhill
(125 hectares/305 acres) and Deveron Forest
(75 hectares/185 acres). The forests we manage
contain more than 3.5 times the number of trees
employed each year in making paper for the books
we manufacture.

Because of this ongoing ecological investment
programme, you, as our customer, can have the
pleasure and reassurance of knowing that a tree
is being cultivated on your behalf to naturally
replace the materials used to make the book you
are holding.

Our forestry programme is run in accordance with
the UK Woodland Assurance Scheme (UKWAS) and
will be certified by the internationally recognized
Forest Stewardship Council (FSC). The FSC is a non-
government organization dedicated to promoting
responsible management of the world's forests.
Certification ensures forests are managed in an
environmentally sustainable and socially responsible
way. For further information about this scheme,
go to www.annesspublishing.com/trees

PUBLISHER'S NOTE

Although the advice and information in this book are
believed to be accurate and true at the time of going
to press, neither the authors nor the publisher can
accept any legal responsibility or liability for any
errors or omissions that may have been made nor for
any inaccuracies nor for any loss, harm or injury that
comes about from following instructions or advice in
this book.

**Main image on front cover shows Skate Salad
with Mustard, Garlic and Soy Dressing. For the
recipe, see page 48.**

NOTES

Bracketed terms are intended for American
readers.
For all recipes, quantities are given in both
metric and imperial measures and, where
appropriate, in standard cups and spoons. Follow
one set of measures, but not a mixture, because
they are not interchangeable.

Standard spoon and cup measures are level. 1
tsp = 5ml, 1 tbsp = 15ml, 1 cup = 250ml/8fl oz.

Australian standard tablespoons are 20ml.
Australian readers should use 3 tsp in place of 1
tbsp for measuring small quantities.

American pints are 16fl oz/2 cups. American
readers should use 20fl oz/2.5 cups in place of 1
pint when measuring liquids.

Electric oven temperatures in this book are for
conventional ovens. When using a fan oven, the
temperature will probably need to be reduced by
about 10–20°C/20–40°F. Since ovens vary, you
should check with your manufacturer's
instruction book for guidance.

Medium (US large) eggs are used unless
otherwise stated.

Contents

Introduction

Salads are enjoyed in most countries of the world. The appeal of salad dishes owes much to their versatility: they can be served warm or cold, as appetizers, side dishes, main courses or even desserts. And there is no limit to the variations possible.

HISTORY OF SALADS

The name 'salad' originates from the word 'sal', meaning 'salt'. Vegetables were seasoned with brine or salted oil and vinegar, hence the name 'salata' or 'salted herb'. The first salads in classical times were green leaves tossed into a dressing. Over the centuries they have been added to and embellished, but salads still start off with the same basic formula, or a variation of that original recipe. Now, there is a huge range of ingredients and recipes to choose from so the creative cook will never be short of inspiration when making a salad.

SIDE, GREEN AND VEGETABLE SALADS

Green side salads generally include torn up leaves and lettuces, with chopped herbs and a dressing.

Any seasonal vegetables can be used to make a salad. Avocados, broccoli, beetroot (beets), beansprouts, tomatoes, cucumber, spring onions (scallions), radishes, olives, red onions, artichoke hearts, green beans, broad (fava) beans, peas, celery, carrots and red or yellow (bell) peppers are all common ingredients. Roasted vegetables are also becoming popular in salads, and with the addition of a few chopped herbs and a dressing of extra virgin olive oil and balsamic vinegar poured on when they are still warm, they are delicious as a side salad with grilled or roasted meat or poultry.

MEAT AND GRAIN SALADS

To make a substantial main course salad, include a protein food such as cheese, eggs, nuts, seeds, fish, beans, meat or poultry. The addition of grains such as rice or pasta, couscous, quinoa and bulgur makes a more satisfying salad, and some Middle Eastern cuisines add pieces of toasted flat bread. Potatoes and starchy vegetables such as pumpkin are often made into a salad on their own. Different countries have their own individual versions for many salads,

LEFT: *Prawns, scallops and squid with Thai flavourings make a luscious salad.*

ABOVE: *Duck skewers are griddled and served with mushrooms in this salad.*

ABOVE: *Asian salads can be made from raw and cooked vegetables with spicy sauce.*

ABOVE: *Meats such as venison can be combined with fruit for a taste sensation.*

and the recipe is adapted to suit the ingredients and tastes of the people there. However, all good salads should include fresh, raw (or lightly cooked) vegetables and/or fruits, making them tasty and nutritious. Sometimes garnishes add colour, flavour or texture. They can include diced cheese, chopped bacon, nuts, croûtons, anchovies, seeds, berries, shredded carrots or cress.

FRUIT SALADS

These vary according to season and availability and tend to be a mix of fresh fruit in season, either chopped or sliced on a platter, or stewed if the fruit cannot be eaten raw, or alternatively, dried or candied fruits. Fruit salads are eaten in various forms all over the world.

DRESSINGS

These are the sauces added to salads and they vary from country to country. A popular version is vinaigrette dressing, which is a mixture of oil and vinegar with the addition of herbs and mustard and sometimes spices. Mayonnaise-type dressings are based on oil and egg yolks, sometimes with yogurt, crème fraîche or sour cream added, or cooked salad cream dressings with eggs. There are numerous dressings for potato salad, which vary from country to country; in Germany it is always made with mustard and vinegar, but no mayonnaise, whereas in the UK and USA, it usually includes a dressing of mayonnaise. In Asian countries, dressings commonly use ingredients such as soy sauce, fish sauce and sesame oil.

This book provides some fantastic recipes for all types of salads using a creative array of ingredients such as vegetables, fruit, rice, grains, meat, fish and poultry. Whatever you feel like, whether it is a quick snack or a satisfying meal, a side dish or a selection of salads for a buffet, there is sure to be a salad recipe to fit each and every occasion.

Vegetable Salads

A crunchy salad makes an excellent

appetizer or light meal. You'll never be

bored with salads – they are endlessly

versatile and can be made with myriad

ingredients of your choice, such as

cheeses, tofu, beans and grains. The salads

in this section are drawn from many regions

of the world, but they all have wonderful

flavours and are prepared with the

freshest ingredients.

Warm vegetable salad with peanut sauce

Based on the classic Indonesian salad gado-gado, this salad features raw red pepper and sprouted beans, which make a crunchy contrast to the warm steamed broccoli, green beans and carrots. Topped with slices of hard-boiled egg, this salad is substantial enough to serve as a main course.

SERVES 2–4

8 new potatoes
225g/8oz broccoli, cut into small florets
200g/7oz/1½ cups fine green beans
2 carrots, cut into thin ribbons with
    a vegetable peeler
1 red (bell) pepper, seeded and cut into strips
50g/2oz/½ cup beansprouts
sprigs of watercress or parsley, to garnish

FOR THE PEANUT SAUCE
15ml/1 tbsp sunflower oil
1 bird's-eye chilli, seeded and sliced

1 garlic clove, crushed
5ml/1 tsp ground coriander
5ml/1 tsp ground cumin
60ml/4 tbsp crunchy peanut butter
15ml/1 tbsp dark soy sauce
1cm/½in piece fresh root ginger,
    finely grated
5ml/1 tsp soft dark brown sugar
15ml/1 tbsp lime juice
60ml/4 tbsp coconut milk

1 To make the peanut sauce, heat the oil in a pan. Add the chilli and garlic, and cook for 1 minute or until softened. Add the spices and cook for a further minute. Stir in the peanut butter and 75ml/5 tbsp water, then cook for 2 minutes until combined, stirring constantly.

2 Add the soy sauce, ginger, sugar, lime juice and coconut milk, then cook gently over low heat until smooth and heated through, stirring frequently. Transfer the mixture to a bowl.

3 Bring a pan of lightly salted water to the boil, add the potatoes and cook for 10–15 minutes, until tender. Drain, then halve or thickly slice the potatoes, depending on their size. Meanwhile, steam the broccoli and green beans for 4–5 minutes until tender but still crisp. Add the carrots 2 minutes before the end of the cooking time.

4 Arrange the cooked vegetables on a serving platter with the red pepper and beansprouts. Garnish with watercress or parsley and serve immediately with the peanut sauce.

Nutritional information per portion: Energy 253kcal/1057kJ; Protein 9.6g; Carbohydrate 28.3g, of which sugars 11.4g; Fat 11.9g, of which saturates 2.6g; Cholesterol 0mg; Calcium 79mg; Fibre 5.9g; Sodium 360mg.

Leek and red pepper salad with goat's cheese

The contrasting textures of silky, grilled peppers, soft cheese and slightly crisp leeks makes this salad extra-specially delicious. This makes a good first course served with crusty bread.

SERVES 6

4 x 1cm/½in thick slices French goat's
    cheese log (chèvre)
65g/2½oz/1 cup fine dry white
    breadcrumbs
675g/1½lb young leeks, trimmed
15ml/1 tbsp olive oil
2 large red (bell) peppers, halved
    and seeded
few sprigs fresh thyme, chopped
vegetable oil, for shallow frying
45ml/3 tbsp chopped fresh flat
    leaf parsley
salt and ground black pepper

FOR THE DRESSING

75ml/5 tbsp extra virgin olive oil
1 small garlic clove, finely chopped
5ml/1 tsp Dijon mustard, plain or
    flavoured with herbes de Provence
15ml/1 tbsp red wine vinegar

1 Remove any skin from the cheese and roll the slices in the breadcrumbs, pressing them in so that the cheese is well coated. Chill the cheese for 1 hour.

2 Cook the leeks in boiling water for 3–4 minutes. Drain and cut into 7.5cm/3in lengths and toss in the oil and seasoning. Grill (broil) them for 3 minutes on each side.

3 Grill the peppers, skin side up, until the skin is blistered. Place in a bowl, cover and leave for 10 minutes, so that they soften. Remove the skin then slice the flesh. Add to the leeks and thyme, adding pepper to taste.

4 Make the dressing by shaking all the ingredients together in a jar, adding seasoning to taste. Pour the dressing over the salad and chill it for several hours. Bring the salad back to room temperature before serving.

5 When ready to serve, heat a shallow layer of vegetable oil in a non-stick frying pan and fry the goat's cheeses quickly until golden brown on each side. Drain them on kitchen paper and cool slightly, then cut into bite-size pieces. Toss the cheese and parsley into the salad and serve immediately.

Nutritional information per portion: Energy 266kcal/1105kJ; Protein 5.8g; Carbohydrate 17.1g, of which sugars 6.6g; Fat 19.8g, of which saturates 3.9g; Cholesterol 8mg; Calcium 60mg; Fibre 3.7g; Sodium 175mg.

Aubergine salad with shrimp and egg

This is an appetizing and unusual salad, from Thailand, that you will find yourself making over and over again. Roasting the aubergines adds a different dimension to their subtle flavour.

SERVES 4–6

2 aubergines (eggplants)
15ml/1 tbsp vegetable oil
30ml/2 tbsp dried shrimp, soaked in
    warm water for 10 minutes
15ml/1 tbsp coarsely chopped garlic
1 hard-boiled egg, chopped
4 shallots, thinly sliced into rings
fresh coriander (cilantro) leaves and
    2 fresh red chillies, seeded and sliced,
    to garnish

FOR THE DRESSING

30ml/2 tbsp fresh lime juice
5ml/1 tsp palm sugar (jaggery) or
    light muscovado (brown) sugar
30ml/2 tbsp Thai fish sauce

1 Preheat the oven to 180°C/350°F/ Gas 4. Prick the aubergines with a skewer, then arrange on a baking sheet. Roast for about 1 hour, turning at least twice, until charred and tender. Remove and set aside until cool enough to handle. Then peel off the skin and cut the flesh into slices.

2 Meanwhile, make the dressing. Put the lime juice, sugar and fish sauce into a bowl. Whisk well with a fork. Cover with clear film (plastic wrap) and set aside until required.

3 Heat the oil in a small frying pan. Drain the shrimp and add to the pan with the garlic. Cook over a medium heat for 3 minutes, until golden. Remove from the pan and set aside.

4 Carefully arrange the roasted aubergine slices on a serving dish. Top with the hard-boiled egg, shallots and dried shrimp mixture.

5 Drizzle the dressing over the salad. Garnish with coriander and sliced chillies.

Nutritional information per portion: Energy 90kcal/376kJ; Protein 7.2g; Carbohydrate 4.7g, of which sugars 4.3g; Fat 4.9g, of which saturates 0.9g; Cholesterol 86mg; Calcium 113mg; Fibre 3g; Sodium 612mg.

Aubergine salad with dried shrimp

The mild flavour of the aubergines in this appetizing and unusual Thai salad is enlivened by the addition of garlic and shrimp and lime juice, fish sauce, fresh chillies and coriander.

SERVES 4–6

2 aubergines (eggplants)

15ml/1 tbsp vegetable oil

30ml/2 tbsp dried shrimp, soaked for
    10 minutes and drained

15ml/1 tbsp chopped garlic

1 hard-boiled egg, chopped

4 shallots, thinly sliced into rings

fresh coriander (cilantro) leaves and
    2 fresh red chillies, seeded and sliced,
    to garnish

FOR THE DRESSING

30ml/2 tbsp lime juice

5ml/1 tsp palm sugar (jaggery) or light
    muscovado (brown) sugar

30ml/2 tbsp fish sauce

1 Grill (broil) or roast the aubergines in a preheated oven, 180°C/350°F/ Gas 4, until charred and tender. Leave the aubergines until they are cool enough to handle, then peel off the skins and slice the flesh.

2 Heat the oil in a small frying pan, add the drained shrimp and garlic and cook over a low heat, stirring frequently, for 3–4 minutes, until golden. Remove from the pan and set aside.

3 To make the dressing, put the lime juice, sugar and fish sauce in a small bowl and whisk together until combined.

4 To serve, arrange the aubergines on a serving dish. Top with the egg, shallots and dried shrimp mixture. Drizzle over the dressing and garnish with coriander and chillies. Serve the salad immediately.

Nutritional information per portion: Energy 91kcal/380kJ; Protein 7.3g; Carbohydrate 4.8g, of which sugars 4.5g; Fat 4.9g, of which saturates 0.9g; Cholesterol 85mg; Calcium 116mg; Fibre 3.2g; Sodium 347mg.

Chinese leaves in kimchi dressing

In this Korean salad, the Chinese leaves have a natural sweetness and delicious crisp texture which is complemented by the spiciness of a traditional kimchi dressing.

SERVES 4

1 head Chinese leaves
  (Chinese cabbage)
25g/1oz/2 tbsp salt
10g/¹⁄₄oz/2¹⁄₂ tsp short grain rice or
  pudding rice
2 leeks, finely sliced
1 white onion, finely sliced
115g/4oz spring onions (scallions),
  roughly chopped
15ml/1 tbsp sesame seeds

FOR THE DRESSING

50g/2oz Korean chilli powder
¹⁄₂ white onion, finely grated
15ml/1 tbsp fermented shrimps, finely
  chopped
30ml/2 tbsp anchovy sauce
2 garlic cloves, crushed
7.5ml/1¹⁄₂ tsp grated fresh root ginger

1 Cut the head of Chinese leaves lengthways into quarters. Place in a bowl and sprinkle with the salt. Leave to stand for 30 minutes and then drain off any liquid that has collected in the bowl.

2 Place the rice in a small pan with 50ml/2fl oz/¹⁄₄ cup water and simmer over a low heat, stirring often, until it has a smooth, milky texture.

3 For the dressing, mix the chilli powder, onion, shrimps, anchovy sauce, garlic and ginger in a bowl, then add the rice. Stir gently to mix.

4 Slice off the core from the Chinese leaves and separate the leaves. Place the leaves in a large bowl.

5 Add the leeks, white onion and spring onions to the bowl, and pour over the dressing. Mix thoroughly so that the leaves are well coated with the dressing. Garnish with sesame seeds and serve.

Nutritional information per portion: Energy 90kcal/377kJ; Protein 5.8g; Carbohydrate 9.2g, of which sugars 5.2g; Fat 3.5g, of which saturates 0.6g; Cholesterol 19mg; Calcium 134mg; Fibre 3.8g; Sodium 169mg.

Fried tofu salad with a tangy sauce

A favourite at hawker stalls in Malaysia, fried tofu can either be stuffed with beansprouts and cucumber and then drizzled with a sauce, or it can be arranged as a salad on a plate. Either way, this salad is tangy and refreshing, an ideal accompaniment to grilled meats and noodles.

SERVES 4

vegetable oil, for deep-frying
450g/1lb firm rectangular tofu, rinsed,
    patted dry and cut into blocks of 5 x 1 cm/
    2 x ½ in
1 small cucumber, partially peeled in strips,
    seeded and shredded
2 spring onions (scallions), trimmed, halved
    and shredded
2 handfuls of fresh beansprouts, rinsed
    and drained
fresh coriander (cilantro) leaves, to garnish

FOR THE SAUCE

30ml/2 tbsp tamarind pulp, soaked in water
    until soft
15ml/1 tbsp sesame or groundnut
    (peanut) oil
4 shallots, finely chopped
4 garlic cloves, finely chopped
2 red chillies, seeded
2.5ml/½ tsp shrimp paste
115g/4oz/1 cup roasted peanuts, crushed
30–45ml/2–3 tbsp kecap manis
15ml/1 tbsp tomato ketchup

1 First make the sauce. Squeeze the tamarind pulp to soften it in the water, and then strain through a sieve (strainer). Measure out 120ml/4fl oz/½ cup tamarind pulp.

2 Heat the sesame or groundnut oil in a wok or heavy pan, and stir in the shallots, garlic and chillies, until fragrant. Stir in the shrimp paste and the peanuts, until they emit a nutty aroma. Add the kecap manis, tomato ketchup and tamarind pulp and blend to form a thick sauce. Set aside and leave to cool.

3 Heat enough oil for deep-frying in a wok or heavy pan. Slip in the blocks of tofu and fry until golden brown all over. Pat dry on kitchen paper and cut each block into slices. Arrange the slices on a plate with the cucumber, spring onions and beansprouts. Drizzle the sauce over the top or serve it separately in a bowl and garnish with the coriander leaves.

Nutritional information per portion: Energy 423kcal/1749kJ; Protein 17.9g; Carbohydrate 7.8g, of which sugars 4.5g; Fat 35.8g, of which saturates 5.3g; Cholesterol 0mg; Calcium 607mg; Fibre 2.8g; Sodium 296mg.

Avocado, red onion and spinach salad with polenta croûtons

The simple lemon dressing gives a sharp tang to the creamy avocado, sweet red onions and crisp spinach leaves. Crunchy golden polenta croûtons, with their soft centre, add a delicious contrast.

SERVES 4

1 large red onion, cut into wedges
300g/11oz ready-made polenta,
   cut into 1cm/¹⁄₂in cubes
olive oil, for brushing
225g/8oz baby spinach leaves
1 avocado
5ml/1 tsp lemon juice

FOR THE DRESSING
60ml/4 tbsp extra virgin olive oil
juice of ¹⁄₂ lemon
salt and ground black pepper

1 Preheat the oven to 200°C/400°F/Gas 6. Place the onion wedges and polenta cubes on a lightly oiled baking sheet and bake for 25 minutes or until the onion is tender and the polenta is crisp and golden, turning them regularly to prevent them sticking. Leave to cool slightly.

2 Meanwhile, make the dressing. Put the olive oil, lemon juice and seasoning to taste in a bowl or screw-top jar. Stir or shake thoroughly to combine.

3 Put the baby spinach leaves in a serving bowl. Peel, stone (pit) and slice the avocado, and toss the slices in the lemon juice to prevent them browning. Add to the spinach with the roasted onions.

4 Pour the dressing over the salad and toss gently to combine. Sprinkle the polenta croûtons on top or hand them around separately, and serve immediately.

Nutritional information per portion: Energy 445kcal/1849kJ; Protein 8.1g; Carbohydrate 48.3g, of which sugars 1.8g; Fat 23.9g, of which saturates 3.5g; Cholesterol 0mg; Calcium 104mg; Fibre 3.6g; Sodium 81mg.

Fried egg salad

Chillies and eggs may seem unlikely partners, but work very well together. The peppery taste of the watercress makes it ideal for this salad, but you could also use rocket (arugula).

SERVES 2

15ml/1 tbsp groundnut (peanut) oil
1 garlic clove, thinly sliced
4 eggs
2 shallots, thinly sliced
2 small fresh red chillies, seeded and
    thinly sliced
1/2 small cucumber, finely diced
1cm/1/2in piece fresh root ginger,
    peeled and grated
juice of 2 limes
30ml/2 tbsp soy sauce
5ml/1 tsp caster (superfine) sugar
a small bunch of coriander (cilantro)
a bunch of watercress or rocket (arugula),
    coarsely chopped

1 Heat the oil in a frying pan. Add the garlic and cook over a low heat until it starts to turn golden. Crack in the eggs. Break the yolks with a wooden spatula, then fry until the eggs are almost firm. Remove from the pan and set aside.

2 Mix the shallots, chillies, cucumber and ginger in a bowl. In a separate bowl, whisk the lime juice with the soy sauce and sugar, pour over the vegetables and toss lightly.

3 Chop the coriander sprigs and add them to the salad. Toss it again to mix thoroughly.

4 Reserve a few watercress sprigs for the garnish and arrange the rest on the base of two serving plates. Cut the eggs into slices and divide them between the watercress mounds. Spoon the shallot mixture all over the salad and serve, garnished with watercress sprigs or rocket.

Nutritional information per portion: Energy 215kcal/894kJ; Protein 14.2g; Carbohydrate 2.4g, of which sugars 2.2g; Fat 16.9g, of which saturates 4.2g; Cholesterol 381mg; Calcium 112mg; Fibre 0.8g; Sodium 1223mg.

Quail's egg salad with cheese

For this recipe, choose a full-fat soft cheese that has a rich and creamy taste. Together with the soft eggs and crunchy pine nuts, this creates a luxurious combination of flavours.

SERVES 4

8 quail's eggs
vinegar, for poaching
1/2 red onion, finely chopped
1/2 leek, cut into fine strips and blanched
75g/3oz full-flavoured full-fat soft cheese, finely diced
1/2 red cabbage, shredded
a handful of mixed salad leaves, including Little Gem (Bibb) lettuce and lollo bionda
10ml/2 tsp pine nuts
salad dressing

1 Poach the quail's eggs. To a pan of simmering water add a dash of vinegar. Break an egg and put it into an eggcup. Gently lower the cup into the simmering water, allowing some water to cover and firm up the egg, then slide it into the water and cook for about 2 minutes.

2 The white should change from transparent to just white and firm. Lift the egg out with a slotted spoon and put it into a bowl of iced water.

2 When all the eggs are cooked lift them out of the water and dry them on kitchen paper. This last bit can be done just before you assemble the salad since the quail's eggs will keep in cold water for up to two days.

3 Combine the salad ingredients, including the pine nuts (which can be lightly toasted if you like). Toss with your chosen dressing. To serve, simply place the diced cheese and the quail's eggs on top of the salad.

Nutritional information per portion: Energy 231kcal/956kJ; Protein 11.7g; Carbohydrate 5.3g, of which sugars 4.8g; Fat 17.7g, of which saturates 5.6g; Cholesterol 132mg; Calcium 203mg; Fibre 2.3g; Sodium 183mg.

Quinoa salad with citrus dressing

Quinoa is a type of grain grown in the Andes that has been cultivated since the time of the Incas and Aztecs. Quinoa is packed with protein and is also gluten free, so it is ideal for vegetarians and those who are gluten-intolerant. As it has a fairly bland flavour, a flavourful dressing is needed.

SERVES 6

175g/6oz/1 cup quinoa
¹/₂ cucumber, peeled
1 large tomato, seeded and cubed
4 spring onions (scallions), sliced
30ml/2 tbsp chopped fresh mint
15ml/1 tbsp chopped fresh flat
    leaf parsley
salt

FOR THE DRESSING
90ml/6 tbsp olive oil
juice of 2 limes
juice of 1 large orange
2 fresh green chillies, seeded and
    finely chopped
2 garlic cloves, crushed

1 Put the quinoa in a sieve (strainer), rinse thoroughly under cold water, then transfer to a large pan. Pour in cold water to cover and bring to the boil. Lower the heat and simmer for 10–12 minutes, until tender. Drain and leave to cool.

2 Make a dressing by whisking the oil with the citrus juices. Stir in the chillies and garlic and season with salt.

3 Cut the cucumber in half lengthways and, using a teaspoon, scoop out and discard the seeds. Cut into 5mm/¹/₄in slices and add to the cooled quinoa with the tomato, spring onions and herbs. Toss well to combine.

4 Pour the dressing over the salad and toss again until well mixed. Check the seasoning and serve.

Nutritional information per portion: Energy 213kcal/885kJ; Protein 3.4g; Carbohydrate 24.3g, of which sugars 2g; Fat 11.6g, of which saturates 1.6g; Cholesterol 0mg; Calcium 26mg; Fibre 0.5g; Sodium 5mg.

Couscous salad

Couscous salad is popular almost everywhere nowadays. In Morocco, as you would expect, there are many ways of serving couscous – this salad has a delicate flavour and is excellent served with any type of tagine, or with grilled chicken, fish or vegetables, or with meat kebabs.

SERVES 4

275g/10oz/1²/₃ cups couscous

525ml/18fl oz/2¹/₄ cups boiling
   vegetable stock

16–20 black olives

2 small courgettes (zucchini)

25g/1oz/¹/₄ cup flaked (sliced)
   almonds, toasted

FOR THE DRESSING

60ml/4 tbsp olive oil

15ml/1 tbsp lemon juice

15ml/1 tbsp chopped fresh
   coriander (cilantro)

15ml/1 tbsp chopped fresh parsley

good pinch of ground cumin

good pinch of cayenne pepper

salt

1 Place the couscous in a bowl and pour over the boiling stock. Stir with a fork and then set aside for 10 minutes. Fluff up with a fork.

2 Halve the olives, discarding the stones (pits). Top and tail the courgettes and cut into small julienne strips.

3 Carefully mix the courgettes, olives and almonds into the couscous.

4 For the dressing, blend together the olive oil, lemon juice, herbs, spices and a pinch of salt and stir into the salad.

COOK'S TIP

If preferred, you can reconstitute the pre-cooked couscous by steaming it.

Nutritional information per portion: Energy 324kcal/1344kJ; Protein 7.1g; Carbohydrate 37.4g, of which sugars 1.8g; Fat 17g, of which saturates 2.1g; Cholesterol 0mg; Calcium 80mg; Fibre 2.1g; Sodium 287mg.

Potato and feta salad

This is an easy dish to assemble, so it makes a perfect lunch or dinner for a busy day. Potato salad is sometimes bland, but this one has layer upon layer of flavour.

SERVES 4

500g/1¼lb small new potatoes
5 spring onions (scallions), green and white parts, finely chopped
15ml/1 tbsp rinsed bottled capers
8–10 black olives
115g/4oz feta cheese, cut into small cubes
45ml/3 tbsp finely chopped fresh flat leaf parsley
30ml/2 tbsp finely chopped fresh mint
salt and ground black pepper

FOR THE VINAIGRETTE

90–120ml/6–8 tbsp extra virgin olive oil
juice of 1 lemon, or to taste
2 salted or preserved anchovies, rinsed and finely chopped
45ml/3 tbsp Greek (US strained plain) yogurt
45ml/3 tbsp finely chopped fresh dill
5ml/1 tsp French mustard

1 Bring a pan of lightly salted water to the boil and cook the potatoes in their skins for 25–30 minutes, until tender. Take care not to let them become soggy and disintegrate. Drain them thoroughly and let them cool a little.

2 When the potatoes are cool enough to handle, peel them and place in a large mixing bowl. If they are very small, keep them whole; otherwise cut them in large cubes. Add the spring onions, capers, olives, feta and fresh herbs and toss gently to mix.

3 To make the vinaigrette, place the oil in a bowl with the lemon juice and the chopped anchovies.

4 Whisk thoroughly until the dressing emulsifies and thickens. Whisk in the yogurt, dill and mustard, with salt and pepper to taste.

5 Dress the salad while the potatoes are still warm, tossing lightly to coat everything in the anchovy vinaigrette. The salad tastes better if it has had time to sit for an hour or so at room temperature and absorb all the flavours before it is served. Any leftover salad will be delicious the next day, but take it out of the refrigerator about an hour before it is to be served or the flavours will be dulled.

Nutritional information per portion: Energy 397kcal/1651kJ; Protein 10g; Carbohydrate 25.4g, of which sugars 6.7g; Fat 29.2g, of which saturates 7.3g; Cholesterol 22mg; Calcium 241mg; Fibre 1.7g; Sodium 489mg.

Griddled halloumi and bean salad with skewered potatoes

Halloumi is a hard, white, salty goat's milk cheese that squeaks when you bite it. It cooks really well and is the perfect complement to the lovely, fresh flavours of the vegetables. For this salad it can be cooked either on the stovetop or on the barbecue.

SERVES 4

20 baby new potatoes, total weight about
   300g/11oz
200g/7oz extra fine green beans, trimmed
675g/1½lb broad (fava) beans, shelled
   (shelled weight about 225g/8oz)
200g/7oz halloumi cheese, cut into 5mm/
   ¼in slices
1 garlic clove, crushed to a paste with a large
   pinch of salt

90ml/6 tbsp olive oil
5ml/1 tsp cider vinegar or white wine vinegar
15g/½ oz/ ½ cup fresh basil
   leaves, shredded
45ml/3 tbsp chopped fresh savory
2 spring onions (scallions), finely sliced
salt and ground black pepper

1 Thread the potatoes on to 4 skewers, and cook in salted boiling water for about 7 minutes. Add the green beans and cook for 3 minutes more, then cook the broad beans for 2 minutes. Drain all the vegetables. Refresh the broad beans under cold water. Pop each out of its skin and discard the skins. Put the beans in a bowl, cover and set aside.

2 Place the halloumi slices and the potato skewers in a wide dish. Whisk the garlic and oil together with black pepper. Add to the dish and toss the halloumi and potato skewers in the mixture.

3 Prepare a barbecue, and place a griddle on a rack over it, or heat a griddle on the stovetop. When the griddle is hot, place the cheese and potato skewers on it and cook for about 2 minutes on each side.

4 Add the vinegar to the oil and garlic remaining in the dish and whisk to mix. Toss in the beans, herbs and spring onions, with the cooked halloumi. Serve, with the potato skewers laid alongside.

Nutritional information per portion: Energy 393kcal/1635kJ; Protein 16.5g; Carbohydrate 20.8g, of which sugars 3.4g; Fat 27.7g, of which saturates 9.4g; Cholesterol 29mg; Calcium 263mg; Fibre 6.3g; Sodium 215mg.

Bean salad

Salads made with haricot, soya, borlotti or black-eyed beans are popular as meze dishes, or as accompaniments to grilled meats. Whether they are simple salads or more elaborate, they make a tasty, healthy, and delicious lunch dish.

SERVES FOUR

225g/8oz/1 ¼ cups dried haricot (navy), soya or black-eyed beans (peas), soaked in cold water for at least 6 hours or overnight

1 red onion, cut in half lengthways, in half again crossways, and sliced along the grain

45–60ml/3–4 tbsp black olives, drained

a bunch of fresh flat leaf parsley, chopped

60ml/4 tbsp olive oil

juice of 1 lemon

3–4 eggs, boiled until just firm, shelled and quartered

12 canned or bottled anchovy fillets, rinsed and drained

salt and ground black pepper

lemon wedges, to serve

1 Drain the beans, transfer them to a pan and fill the pan with plenty of cold water. Bring the water to the boil and boil the beans for 1 minute, then lower the heat and partially cover the pan. Depending on the variety of beans used, simmer for about 45 minutes, until the beans are cooked but still firm – they should have a bite to them, and not be soft and mushy.

2 Drain the beans, rinse well under cold running water and remove any skins.

3 Mix the beans in a wide, shallow bowl with the onion, olives and most of the parsley. Toss in the oil and lemon juice, and season with salt and pepper.

4 Place the eggs and anchovy fillets on top of the salad and add the remaining parsley. Serve with lemon wedges.

Nutritional information per portion: Energy 402kcal/1674kJ; Protein 28g; Carbohydrate 10.4g, of which sugars 4.2g; Fat 28g, of which saturates 4.4g; Cholesterol 149mg; Calcium 221mg; Fibre 10g; Sodium 696mg.

White beans with green peppers in spicy dressing

Tender white beans are delicious in this spicy sauce with the bite of fresh, crunchy green pepper. The dish was brought to Israel by the Jews of Balkan lands, such as Turkey, Bulgaria and Greece. It is perfect for preparing ahead of time.

SERVES 4

750g/1²/₃lb tomatoes, diced

1 onion, finely chopped

¹/₂–1 mild fresh chilli, finely chopped

1 green (bell) pepper, seeded and
   chopped

pinch of sugar

4 garlic cloves, chopped

400g/14oz can cannellini beans, drained

45–60ml/3–4 tbsp olive oil

grated rind and juice of 1 lemon

15ml/1 tbsp cider vinegar or wine vinegar

salt and ground black pepper

chopped fresh parsley, to garnish

1 Put the tomatoes, onion, chilli, green pepper, sugar, garlic, cannellini beans, salt and plenty of ground black pepper in a large bowl and toss together until well combined.

2 Add the olive oil, grated lemon rind, lemon juice and vinegar to the salad and toss lightly to combine. Chill before serving, garnished with the chopped parsley.

Nutritional information per portion: Energy 226kcal/947kJ; Protein 8.8g; Carbohydrate 27.6g, of which sugars 12.9g; Fat 9.6g, of which saturates 1.5g; Cholesterol 0mg; Calcium 92mg; Fibre 9g; Sodium 409mg.

Warm black-eyed bean salad with rocket

This is an easy dish as black-eyed beans do not need to be soaked overnight. By adding spring onions and a generous quantity of aromatic dill, they are transformed to a refreshing and healthy salad. It can be served hot or at room temperature.

SERVES 4

275g/10oz/1 ½ cups black-eyed
   beans (peas)
5 spring onions (scallions), sliced
a large handful of rocket (arugula) leaves,
   chopped if large
45–60ml/3–4 tbsp chopped fresh dill
150ml/¼ pint/⅔ cup extra virgin
   olive oil
juice of 1 lemon, or more
10–12 black olives
salt and ground black pepper
small cos (romaine) lettuce leaves,
   to serve

1 Rinse and drain the beans, put them into a pan and pour in cold water to cover. Bring to the boil and immediately strain. Put them back in the pan with fresh cold water to cover and add a pinch of salt – this will make their skins harder and stop them from disintegrating when they are cooked.

2 Bring the beans to the boil, then lower the heat slightly and cook them until they are soft but not mushy. They will take 20–30 minutes, so keep an eye on them.

3 Drain the beans, reserving 75–90ml/5–6 tbsp of the cooking liquid. Transfer the beans to a large salad bowl. Immediately add the remaining ingredients, including the reserved liquid, and mix well. Serve straight away, or cooled slightly, piled on the lettuce leaves.

Nutritional information per portion: Energy 238kcal/1007kJ; Protein 16.1g; Carbohydrate 31g, of which sugars 2.4g; Fat 6.4g, of which saturates 0.9g; Cholesterol 0mg; Calcium 114mg; Fibre 12.3g; Sodium 580mg.

Lentil salad with red onion and garlic

This delicious, garlicky lentil salad is frequently served as an accompaniment to kebabs in street cafés and restaurants, and as an appetizer at home. It can be served warm or cooled. If you feel like making a meal out of this dish, serve it with a generous spoonful of plain yogurt.

SERVES 4

45ml/3 tbsp olive oil

2 red onions, chopped

2 tomatoes, peeled, seeded and chopped

10ml/2 tsp ground turmeric

10ml/2 tsp ground cumin

175g/6oz/¾ cup brown or green lentils, picked over and rinsed

900ml/1½ pints/3¾ cups vegetable stock or water

4 garlic cloves, crushed

a small bunch of fresh coriander (cilantro), finely chopped

salt and ground black pepper

1 lemon, cut into wedges, to serve

1 Heat 30ml/2 tbsp of the oil in a large pan or flameproof casserole and fry the onions until soft. Add the tomatoes, turmeric and cumin, then stir in the lentils. Pour in the stock or water and bring to the boil, then reduce the heat and simmer for about 20 minutes until the lentils are tender and almost all the liquid has been absorbed.

2 In a separate pan, fry the garlic in the remaining oil until brown and frizzled. Toss the garlic into the lentils with the fresh coriander and season to taste. Serve warm or at room temperature, with wedges of lemon for squeezing over.

Nutritional information per portion: Energy 244kcal/1025kJ; Protein 12.3g; Carbohydrate 29.2g, of which sugars 6.6g; Fat 9.5g, of which saturates 1.3g; Cholesterol 0mg; Calcium 78mg; Fibre 6.1g; Sodium 16mg.

Pisto Manchego

This is a rich-flavoured and simple summer vegetable dish, from the poorest and hottest part of Spain, La Mancha. It may be eaten hot, alone or with fried ham and eggs. Canned tuna or hard-boiled eggs can be added to make a substantial salad.

SERVES 4

45–60ml/3–4 tbsp olive oil

2 Spanish (Bermuda) onions, thinly sliced

3 garlic cloves, finely chopped

3 large green (bell) peppers, seeded and chopped

3 large courgettes (zucchini), thinly sliced

5 large ripe tomatoes or 800g/1¾lb canned tomatoes, with juice

60ml/4 tbsp chopped fresh parsley

2 hard-boiled eggs (optional)

30–45ml/2–3 tbsp virgin olive oil (if serving cold)

salt and ground black pepper

1 Heat the oil in a large heavy pan or flameproof casserole and cook the onions and garlic gently, until they are soft.

2 Add the peppers, courgettes and tomatoes. Season and cook gently for 20 minutes.

3 Stir in 30ml/2 tbsp parsley and serve hot, if wished, topped with chopped hard-boiled egg, if using, and more parsley.

4 To serve cold, check the seasoning, adding more if needed, and sprinkle the vegetables with a little virgin olive oil before adding the garnish.

Nutritional information per portion: Energy 196kcal/812kJ; Protein 6.2g; Carbohydrate 21.3g, of which sugars 18.5g; Fat 10g, of which saturates 1.6g; Cholesterol 0mg; Calcium 109mg; Fibre 6.4g; Sodium 25mg.

Broad bean and fresh cheese salad

Broad beans are popular in Peru. They are used in soups, stews and many other dishes, and, when young and freshly picked, are eaten raw as a snack. This is a hearty salad that makes a satisfying first course. It can be made with fresh or frozen beans, but fresh young beans are best.

SERVES 4

250g/9oz small white potatoes
250g/9oz/2 cups shelled broad
   (fava) beans
kernels of 1 fresh corn on the cob or 1
   medium can corn in unsalted water
150g/5oz feta cheese, cut into 1cm/$\frac{1}{2}$in
   dice
15ml/1 tbsp white wine vinegar
45ml/3 tbsp olive oil
1 fresh red or green chilli, seeded and
   finely chopped
salt and ground black pepper
lettuce leaves, to garnish, optional

1 Boil the potatoes for 20 minutes, until tender. Drain and cool for 10 minutes, then slide the skin off and cut into 1cm/$\frac{1}{2}$in dice.

2 Boil the broad beans in lightly salted water for 15 minutes. Drain and allow to cool, then pop them out of their skins. If the beans are young and small you need not do this.

3 If using fresh corn on the cob, boil for 10 minutes, then drain and slice off the kernels with a sharp knife. Leave to cool. If using canned corn, drain it.

4 Mix the potatoes, beans and corn kernels with the cheese and dress with the vinegar, oil and seasoning. Sprinkle with the chilli and serve garnished with lettuce, if using.

Nutritional information per portion: Energy 293kcal/1225kJ; Protein 12.6g; Carbohydrate 24.6g, of which sugars 4.6g; Fat 16.7g, of which saturates 6.5g; Cholesterol 26mg; Calcium 175mg; Fibre 5g; Sodium 620mg.

Lentil, tomato and cheese salad

Lentils and cheese are a natural combination. The small blue-green Puy lentils from France are perfect for salads; flat green Continental lentils or massor dhal lentils from India are also good. Chunks of crumbly feta or a mild goat's milk cheese provide an inviting flavour contrast.

SERVES 6

200g/7oz/scant 1 cup lentils (preferably Puy lentils), soaked for about 3 hours in cold water to cover
1 red onion, chopped
1 bay leaf
60ml/4 tbsp extra virgin olive oil
45ml/3 tbsp chopped fresh parsley
30ml/2 tbsp chopped fresh oregano or marjoram
250g/9oz cherry tomatoes, halved
250g/9oz feta, goat's milk cheese or Caerphilly cheese, crumbled
salt and ground black pepper
30–45ml/2–3 tbsp lightly toasted pine nuts and leaves of chicory or frisée and fresh herbs, to garnish

1 Drain the lentils and place them in a large pan. Pour in plenty of cold water and add the onion and bay leaf. Bring to the boil, then lower the heat and simmer for 20 minutes or according to the instructions on the packet.

2 Drain the lentils, discard the bay leaf and put them into a bowl. Add salt and pepper to taste. Toss with the olive oil. Set aside to cool, then mix with the fresh parsley, oregano or marjoram and cherry tomatoes.

3 Add the cheese. Line a serving dish with chicory or frisée leaves and pile the salad in the centre. Sprinkle over the pine nuts and garnish with fresh herbs.

Nutritional information per portion: Energy 341kcal/1423kJ; Protein 16.1g; Carbohydrate 22g, of which sugars 3.7g; Fat 21.6g, of which saturates 7.2g; Cholesterol 29mg; Calcium 188mg; Fibre 2.7g; Sodium 619mg.

Brown bean salad

Brown beans, which are sometimes called 'ful medames', are widely used in Egyptian cooking, and are occasionally seen in health food shops here. However, dried broad beans and black or red kidney beans make a good substitute.

SERVES 6

350g/12oz/1 ½ cups dried brown beans

3 thyme sprigs

2 bay leaves

1 onion, halved

3 hard-boiled eggs, shelled and roughly chopped

1 pickled cucumber, roughly chopped

FOR THE DRESSING

4 garlic cloves, crushed

7.5ml/1 ½ tsp cumin seeds, crushed

3 spring onions (scallions), finely chopped

90ml/6 tbsp chopped fresh parsley

20ml/4 tsp lemon juice

90ml/6 tbsp olive oil

salt and ground black pepper

1 Put the beans in a bowl with plenty of cold water and leave to soak overnight. Drain, transfer to a large pan and cover with fresh water. Bring to the boil and boil rapidly for 10 minutes.

2 Reduce the heat and add the thyme, bay leaves and onion. Simmer very gently for about 1 hour until tender. Drain and discard the herbs and onion.

3 To make the dressing, mix together the garlic, cumin, spring onions, parsley, lemon juice, oil and add a little salt and pepper. Pour over the beans and toss the ingredients lightly together.

4 Gently stir in the eggs and cucumber and serve at once.

Nutritional information per portion: Energy 300kcal/1258kJ; Protein 16.6g; Carbohydrate 27.1g, of which sugars 2.5g; Fat 14.8g, of which saturates 2.5g; Cholesterol 95mg; Calcium 99mg; Fibre 9.9g; Sodium 50mg.

Green bean and sweet red pepper salad

Because serrano chillies are very fiery, be circumspect about using too many. Use a milder fresh green chilli, if you prefer to accentuate the fresh taste of this crunchy salad.

SERVES 4

350g/12oz cooked green beans, cut into quarters

2 red (bell) peppers, seeded and chopped

2 spring onions (scallions), chopped

1 or more drained pickled serrano chillies, rinsed, seeded and chopped

1 iceberg lettuce, coarsely shredded

olives, to garnish

FOR THE DRESSING

45ml/3 tbsp red wine vinegar

135ml/9 tbsp olive oil

salt and ground black pepper

1 Combine the cooked green beans, chopped peppers, chopped spring onions and chillies in a salad bowl.

2 Make the salad dressing. Pour the red wine vinegar into a bowl or jug (pitcher). Add salt and ground black pepper to taste, then gradually whisk in the olive oil until well combined.

3 Pour the salad dressing over the prepared vegetables and toss lightly together to mix and coat well.

4 Line a large serving platter with the shredded iceberg lettuce leaves and arrange the salad vegetables attractively on top. Garnish with the olives and serve at once.

Nutritional information per portion: Energy 280kcal/1153kJ; Protein 3.1g; Carbohydrate 9.4g, of which sugars 8.4g; Fat 25.8g, of which saturates 3.8g; Cholesterol 0mg; Calcium 55mg; Fibre 3.9g; Sodium 5mg.

Bean salad with tuna and red onion

This makes a great first course or even a light main course if served with a green salad, some garlic mayonnaise and plenty of warm, crusty bread.

SERVES 4

250g/9oz/1¹/₃ cups dried haricot or
    cannellini beans, soaked overnight in
    cold water
1 bay leaf
200–250g/7–9oz fine French green
    beans, trimmed
1 large red onion, very thinly sliced
45ml/3 tbsp chopped fresh flat
    leaf parsley
200–250g/7–9oz good-quality canned
    tuna in olive oil, drained
200g/7oz cherry tomatoes, halved
salt and ground black pepper
a few onion rings, to garnish

FOR THE DRESSING
90ml/6 tbsp extra virgin olive oil
15ml/1 tbsp tarragon vinegar
5ml/1 tsp tarragon mustard
1 garlic clove, finely chopped
5ml/1 tsp grated lemon rind
a little lemon juice

1 Drain the beans and add fresh water and the bay leaf. Boil for 10 minutes. Reduce the heat and simmer for 1¹/₂ hours, until tender. Drain and discard the bay leaf.

2 Put the dressing ingredients, except the lemon juice, in a jug (pitcher) and whisk. Add salt, pepper and lemon juice. Set aside.

3 Blanch the French beans for 3–4 minutes. Drain, refresh under cold water and drain again.

4 Place both types of beans in a bowl. Add half the dressing and toss to mix. Stir in the onion and half the chopped parsley, then season to taste with salt and pepper.

5 Flake the tuna and toss it into the beans with the tomatoes.

6 Arrange the salad on four plates. Drizzle the remaining dressing over the salad and sprinkle the remaining chopped parsley on top. Garnish with a few onion rings and serve.

Nutritional information per portion: Energy 336kcal/1406kJ; Protein 15.2g; Carbohydrate 30.9g, of which sugars 4g; Fat 17.7g, of which saturates 2.6g; Cholesterol 0mg; Calcium 89mg; Fibre 11.5g; Sodium 12mg.

Fish Salads

These diverse salads are made with a variety of fresh fish or smoked fish mixed with salad leaves, potatoes, herbs and exciting dressings.For an elegant supper why not try Asparagus and Smoked Fish Salad or Red Mullet with Raspberry Dressing? If you prefer a simpler family lunch or supper, Whitefish Salad is easy to make, while for the more adventurous, New Year Raw Fish Salad or Turbot Sashimi Salad with Wasabi would be ideal.

Bird's nest salad

This is a particularly attractive dish on the cold table. The ingredients are arranged, as the name suggests, in the shape of a bird's nest encircling a raw egg yolk. All the ingredients, including the yolk, should be stirred together by the first person to help themselves to the dish.

SERVES 4

8 anchovy fillets, roughly chopped
30ml/2 tbsp capers
2 potatoes, cooked, cooled and diced, total quantity 45ml/3 tbsp
45ml/3 tbsp chopped pickled beetroot (beet)
15–30ml/1–2 tbsp finely diced onion
1 very fresh egg

1 Using a medium, round serving dish, place one egg cup in it, upside down. In successive circles around the cup, arrange the anchovies, capers and potatoes. Add the beetroot and onions around the edge of the dish.

2 Carefully remove the egg cup. Break the egg, separating the yolk from the white, and carefully put the whole egg yolk where the egg cups were positioned. Alternatively, you could use an egg shell half to hold the yolk.

Nutritional information per portion: Energy 93kcal/390kJ; Protein 5.9g; Carbohydrate 10.1g, of which sugars 2.3g; Fat 3.6g, of which saturates 0.9g; Cholesterol 99mg; Calcium 41mg; Fibre 0.9g; Sodium 284mg.

COOK'S TIP
Raw egg yolk should not be served to children, the elderly, pregnant women, convalescents or anyone suffering from an illness. The egg must be very fresh.

Whitefish salad

Smoked whitefish is one of the glories of deli food and, made into a salad with mayonnaise and sour cream, it's a good brunch dish. Eat it with a stack of bagels, pumpernickel or rye bread. If you can't find smoked whitefish, use any other smoked firm white fish such as halibut or cod.

SERVES 4–6

1 smoked whitefish, skinned and boned
2 celery sticks, chopped
1/2 red, white or yellow onion or 3–5
  spring onions (scallions), chopped
45ml/3 tbsp mayonnaise
45ml/3 tbsp sour cream or Greek (US
  strained plain) yogurt
juice of 1/2–1 lemon
1 round (butterhead) lettuce
ground black pepper
5–10ml/1–2 tsp chopped fresh parsley, to
  garnish

1 Break the smoked fish into bitesize pieces. In a large bowl, combine the chopped celery, onion or spring onions, mayonnaise, and sour cream or yogurt, and add lemon juice to taste.

2 Fold the fish into the mixture and season with pepper. Arrange the lettuce leaves on serving plates, then spoon the whitefish salad over the top. Serve chilled, sprinkled with parsley.

Nutritional information per portion: Energy 112kcal/469kJ; Protein 10.1g; Carbohydrate 1g, of which sugars 1g; Fat 7.6g, of which saturates 1.9g; Cholesterol 28mg; Calcium 29mg; Fibre 0.3g; Sodium 421mg.

Skate with bitter salad leaves

Skate has a deliciously sweet flavour which is a good match for bitter salad leaves such as escarole, rocket, frisée and radicchio. Serve with toasted French bread.

SERVES 4

800g/1¾lb skate wings
15ml/1 tbsp white wine vinegar
4 black peppercorns
1 fresh thyme sprig
175g/6oz bitter salad leaves, such as
    frisée, rocket (arugula), radicchio,
    escarole and lamb's lettuce
    (corn salad)
1 orange
2 tomatoes, peeled, seeded and diced

FOR THE DRESSING
15ml/1 tbsp white wine vinegar
45ml/3 tbsp olive oil
2 shallots, finely chopped
salt and ground black pepper

1 Put the skate wings into a large shallow pan, cover with cold water and add the vinegar, peppercorns and thyme. Bring to the boil, then poach the fish gently for 8–10 minutes, until the flesh comes away easily from the bones.

2 Meanwhile, make the dressing. Whisk the vinegar, olive oil and shallots together in a bowl. Season to taste. Put the salad leaves into a bowl, pour over the dressing and toss well.

3 Using a zester, remove the outer rind from the orange, then peel it, removing all the pith. Slice into thin rounds.

4 When the skate is cooked, flake the flesh and mix it into the salad. Add the orange rind shreds, the orange slices and tomatoes, toss gently and serve.

Nutritional information per portion: Energy 230kcal/965kJ; Protein 31.6g; Carbohydrate 4.8g, of which sugars 4.8g; Fat 9.5g, of which saturates 1.3g; Cholesterol 0mg; Calcium 118mg; Fibre 1.5g; Sodium 247mg.

Warm monkfish salad

Monkfish has a matchless flavour and benefits from being cooked simply. Teaming it with wilted baby spinach and toasted pine nuts makes an inspirational salad.

SERVES 4

2 monkfish fillets, about 350g/12oz each
25g/1oz/¼ cup pine nuts
15ml/1 tbsp olive oil
15g/½ oz/1 tbsp butter
225g/8oz baby spinach leaves, washed
   and stalks removed
salt and ground black pepper

FOR THE DRESSING
5ml/1 tsp Dijon mustard
5ml/1 tsp sherry vinegar
60ml/4 tbsp olive oil
1 garlic clove, crushed

1 Holding the knife at a slight angle, cut each monkfish fillet into 12 diagonal slices. Season lightly and set aside.

2 Heat an empty frying pan, put in the pine nuts and shake them about for a while, until golden brown. Do not burn. Transfer to a plate; set aside.

3 Whisk the ingredients for the dressing until smooth and creamy. In a small pan, heat the dressing gently and season to taste with salt and pepper.

4 Heat the oil and butter in a frying pan. Sauté the fish for 20 seconds on each side.

5 Put the spinach in a bowl with the warm dressing. Add the pine nuts, reserving a few, and toss well. Divide the spinach among four plates and arrange the fish on top. Sprinkle the reserved pine nuts on top and serve.

Nutritional information per portion: Energy 331kcal/1379kJ; Protein 29.9g; Carbohydrate 1.2g, of which sugars 1.1g; Fat 23g, of which saturates 4.9g; Cholesterol 34mg; Calcium 110mg; Fibre 1.3g; Sodium 137mg.

Hake and potato salad

Hake is a 'meaty' fish that is excellent served cold in a salad. Here the flavour is enhanced with a tasty, piquant dressing of capers and lemon juice.

SERVES 4

450g/1lb hake fillets
150ml/¼ pint/⅔ cup fish stock
1 onion, thinly sliced
1 bay leaf
450g/1lb boiled baby new potatoes
1 red (bell) pepper, seeded and diced
115g/4oz/1 cup petit pois, cooked
2 spring onions (scallions), sliced
½ cucumber, unpeeled and diced
4 large red lettuce leaves
salt and ground black pepper
2 hard-boiled eggs, finely chopped,
    15ml/1 tbsp chopped fresh parsley
    and 15ml/1 tbsp finely chopped fresh
    chives, to garnish

FOR THE DRESSING

150ml/¼ pint/⅔ cup Greek (US
    strained plain) yogurt
30ml/2 tbsp olive oil
juice of ½ lemon
15–30ml/1–2 tbsp capers

1 Put the hake fillets in a large, shallow pan with the fish stock, onion slices and bay leaf.

2 Bring to the boil over a medium heat, lower the heat and poach the fish for about 10 minutes until it flakes easily. Leave it to cool, then remove the skin and any bones and separate the flesh into flakes.

3 Put the baby new potatoes in a bowl with the red pepper, petits pois, spring onions and cucumber.

4 Gently stir in the flaked hake and season with salt and pepper.

5 Make the dressing by stirring all the ingredients together in a bowl or jug (pitcher). Season and spoon or pour over the salad. Toss gently.

6 Place a lettuce leaf on each plate and spoon the salad over it. Mix the finely chopped hard-boiled eggs for the garnish with the parsley and chives. Sprinkle the mixture over each salad.

Nutritional information per portion: Energy 318kcal/1335kJ; Protein 27.8g; Carbohydrate 32.3g, of which sugars 11.7g; Fat 9.6g, of which saturates 1.6g; Cholesterol 26mg; Calcium 134mg; Fibre 4.5g; Sodium 162mg.

Red mullet with raspberry dressing

The combination of red mullet and raspberry vinegar is delicious in this salad. Keep to the red theme by including salad leaves such as red oakleaf lettuce and baby red-stemmed chard.

SERVES 4

8 red mullet or red snapper fillets, scaled

15ml/1 tbsp olive oil

15ml/1 tbsp raspberry vinegar

175g/6oz mixed dark green and red salad leaves, such as lamb's lettuce (corn salad), radicchio, oakleaf lettuce and rocket (arugula)

salt and ground black pepper

FOR THE DRESSING

115g/4oz/1 cup raspberries, puréed and sieved (strained)

30ml/2 tbsp raspberry vinegar

60ml/4 tbsp extra virgin olive oil

2.5ml/¹/₂ tsp caster (superfine) sugar

1 Lay the fish fillets in a shallow dish. Whisk together the olive oil and raspberry vinegar, add a pinch of salt and drizzle the mixture over the fish. Cover and leave to marinate for 1 hour.

2 Meanwhile, whisk together the dressing ingredients and season to taste.

3 Wash and dry the salad leaves, put them in a bowl, pour over most of the dressing and toss lightly.

4 Heat a ridged griddle pan or frying pan until very hot, put in the fish fillets and cook for 2–3 minutes on each side, until just tender. Cut the fillets diagonally in half to make rough diamond shapes.

5 Arrange a tall heap of salad in the middle of each serving plate. Prop up four fish fillet halves on the salad on each plate with the reserved dressing spooned around attractively. Serve the salad immediately.

Nutritional information per portion: Energy 333kcal/1391kJ; Protein 38.2g; Carbohydrate 2.1g, of which sugars 2.1g; Fat 19.2g, of which saturates 1.7g; Cholesterol 0mg; Calcium 152mg; Fibre 1.1g; Sodium 184mg.

Scented fish salad

For a tropical taste of the Far East, try this delicious fish salad scented with coconut, fruit and warm Thai spices. The pitaya or dragon fruit is particularly good with fish.

SERVES 4

350g/12oz fillet of red mullet
1 cos or romaine lettuce
1 each papaya and pitaya, peeled and sliced
1 large ripe tomato, cut into wedges
^{1}/$_2$ cucumber, peeled and cut into batons
3 spring onions (scallions), sliced

FOR THE MARINADE

5ml/1 tsp each coriander and fennel seeds
5ml/1 tsp caster (superfine) sugar
2.5ml/^{1}/$_2$ tsp hot chilli sauce
30ml/2 tbsp garlic oil

FOR THE DRESSING

60ml/4 tbsp coconut milk
60ml/4 tbsp groundnut (peanut) oil
finely grated rind and juice of 1 lime
1 red chilli, seeded and finely chopped
5ml/1 tsp sugar
45ml/3 tbsp chopped fresh
   coriander (cilantro)

1 Cut the fish into even strips, removing any stray bones. Place it on a plate.

2 Make the marinade. Put the coriander and fennel seeds in a mortar. Add the sugar and crush with a pestle to a fine powder. Stir in the chilli sauce, garlic oil, and mix well to form a paste.

3 Spread the paste over the fish, cover and marinate in a cool place for at least 20 minutes.

4 Make the dressing. Place the coconut milk in a jar. Add the oil, lime rind and juice, chilli, sugar and coriander. Shake well.

5 Wash and dry the lettuce leaves. Place in a bowl and add the papaya, pitaya, tomato, cucumber and spring onions. Pour in the dressing and toss well to coat.

6 Heat a large non-stick frying pan, add the fish and cook for 5 minutes, turning once. Add the cooked fish to the salad, toss lightly and serve.

Nutritional information per portion: Energy 304kcal/1269kJ; Protein 17.6g; Carbohydrate 11.7g, of which sugars 11.6g; Fat 21.1g, of which saturates 3.6g; Cholesterol 0mg; Calcium 89mg; Fibre 2.6g; Sodium 88mg.

Fish kebab salad

Any firm-fleshed fish, such as tuna, trout, salmon, monkfish or sea bass, can be used for kebabs, but in Turkey, meaty chunks of swordfish are a favourite.

SERVES 4

500g/1¼lb boneless swordfish loin
or steaks, cut into bitesize chunks
1 lemon, halved lengthways and sliced
1 large tomato, chopped
1 green (bell) pepper, seeded and cut
    into bitesize pieces
a handful of bay leaves
lemon wedges, to serve

FOR THE MARINADE
1 onion, grated
1–2 garlic cloves, crushed
juice of ½ lemon
30–45ml/2–3 tbsp olive oil
5–10ml/1–2 tsp tomato purée (paste)
salt and ground black pepper

1 Mix the marinade ingredients in a shallow bowl. Toss in the chunks of swordfish and set aside for about 30 minutes.

2 Thread the fish on to skewers, alternating with the lemon, tomato and pepper and the occasional bay leaf. If there is any marinade left, brush it over the kebabs.

3 Put a cast-iron griddle pan over a medium heat until very hot. Place the skewers on the pan and cook for 2–3 minutes on each side until the kebab ingredients are quite charred.

4 Serve the kebabs hot with lemon wedges for squeezing.

Nutritional information per portion: Energy 225kcal/940kJ; Protein 23.9g; Carbohydrate 7.8g, of which sugars 7.2g; Fat 11.1g, of which saturates 2g; Cholesterol 51mg; Calcium 18mg; Fibre 1.9g; Sodium 177mg.

Skate salad with mustard, garlic and soy dressing

The sharpness of the mustard and pungency of the garlic offset the flavour of the skate perfectly in this dish. The array of mixed green leaves provide a refreshing addition to this salad.

SERVES 4

800g/1¾ lb skate
15ml/1 tbsp white wine vinegar
15 peppercorns
1 thyme sprig
115g/4oz rocket (arugula)
115g/4oz watercress or rocket
200g/7oz mixed salad leaves
2 tomatoes, seeded and diced
finely pared orange rind, to garnish

FOR THE DRESSING

30ml/2 tbsp grated Asian pear
30ml/2 tbsp virgin olive oil
30ml/2 tbsp white wine vinegar
30ml/2 tbsp crushed garlic
10ml/2 tsp English (hot) mustard
5ml/1 tsp dark soy sauce
salt and ground black pepper

1 Thoroughly rinse the skate in cold water. Bring a large pan of water to the boil and add the vinegar, peppercorns and thyme. Reduce the heat so that the water simmers. Add the skate and poach it for 7–10 minutes, or until the flesh is just beginning to come away from the cartilage. Do not overcook. Drain thoroughly.

2 Remove the skate flesh from the cartilage of the wing. Shred the flesh and set it aside.

3 For the dressing, mix the Asian pear, oil, vinegar, garlic, mustard and soy sauce. Season with salt and pepper and mix well.

4 Place the rocket, watercress or rocket, mixed leaves and diced tomatoes in a large serving bowl. Add the shredded skate and toss the ingredients together.

5 Pour the dressing over the salad, toss lightly and garnish with the orange rind.

Nutritional information per portion: Energy 219kcal/919kJ; Protein 33.6g; Carbohydrate 4.4g, of which sugars 4.2g; Fat 7.5g, of which saturates 1g; Cholesterol 0mg; Calcium 257mg; Fibre 2.8g; Sodium 637mg.

Turbot sashimi salad with wasabi

Sashimi is thinly sliced raw seafood. In Japan, it is served with soy sauce and wasabi; in this Western-inspired salad, a wasabi dressing is used. Wasabi is made from a type of horseradish.

SERVES 4

ice cubes
400g/14oz very fresh thick turbot,
    skinned and filleted
300g/11oz mixed salad leaves
8 radishes, thinly sliced

FOR THE DRESSING
25g/1oz rocket (arugula) leaves
50g/2oz cucumber, chopped
90ml/6 tbsp rice vinegar
75ml/5 tbsp olive oil
5ml/1 tsp salt
15ml/1 tbsp wasabi paste, or the same
    amount of wasabi powder mixed with
    7.5ml/1½ tsp water

1 For the dressing, roughly tear the rocket and mix with the cucumber and vinegar in a food processor. Pour into a bowl and add the rest of the dressing ingredients, except the wasabi. Check the seasoning. Chill.

2 Prepare a bowl of ice-cold water. Cut the turbot in half lengthways, then cut into 5mm/¼in thick slices crossways. Plunge the fish into the ice-cold water as you slice.

3 After 2 minutes or so, the fish slices will start to curl and become firm. Take out with a slotted spoon and drain on kitchen paper.

4 In a large serving bowl, mix the fish, the salad leaves and the radishes together.

5 Mix the wasabi into the dressing, add this to the salad and toss well. Serve immediately.

Nutritional information per portion: Energy 233kcal/969kJ; Protein 18.5g; Carbohydrate 1.8g, of which sugars 1.8g; Fat 16.9g, of which saturates 2.8g; Cholesterol 0mg; Calcium 77mg; Fibre 0.9g; Sodium 72mg.

New Year raw fish salad

To celebrate the lunar New Year, Chinese families get together to eat special dishes, such as this raw fish salad, which all the diners must help to mix with their chopsticks, while they shout 'lo hei' ('toss the fish'), as this ensures good luck and abundance.

SERVES 4–6

175g/6oz fresh tuna or salmon, finely sliced

115g/4oz white fish fillet, finely sliced

25g/1oz fresh root ginger, peeled and finely chopped

2 garlic cloves, crushed

juice of 2 limes

225g/8oz daikon (white radish), cut into julienne strips

2 carrots, cut into julienne strips

1 small cucumber, peeled, seeded and cut into julienne strips

4 spring onions (scallions), trimmed and cut into julienne strips

1 pomelo, segmented and sliced

4 fresh lime leaves, finely sliced

50g/2oz preserved sweet melon, finely sliced

50g/2oz preserved sweet red ginger, finely sliced

ground black pepper

30ml/2 tbsp roasted peanuts, coarsely crushed, to garnish

FOR THE DRESSING

30ml/2 tbsp sesame oil

15ml/1 tbsp light soy sauce

15ml/1 tbsp red wine vinegar

30ml/2 tbsp sour plum sauce

2 garlic cloves, crushed

10ml/2 tsp sugar

1 In a shallow, non-metallic dish, toss the fish in the ginger, garlic and lime juice. Season with black pepper and set aside for at least 30 minutes.

2 Place the daikon, carrots, cucumber, spring onions, pomelo and lime leaves in a large bowl. Add the preserved melon and ginger.

3 In a small bowl, mix together the ingredients for the dressing. Adjust the sweet and sour balance to taste.

4 Just before serving, place the marinated fish on top of the vegetables in the bowl. Pour the dressing over the top and sprinkle with the roasted peanuts. Place the bowl in the middle of the table and let everyone toss the salad with their chopsticks.

Nutritional information per portion: Energy 126kcal/528kJ; Protein 13.2g; Carbohydrate 6.5g, of which sugars 6.4g; Fat 5.4g, of which saturates 1g; Cholesterol 22mg; Calcium 36mg; Fibre 1.3g; Sodium 222mg.

Fresh tuna salad Niçoise

There are many variations of this recipe and fresh tuna transforms this classic and ever-popular colourful salad from the south of France into a more substantial and extra-special dish.

SERVES 4

4 tuna steaks, about 150g/5oz each
30ml/2 tbsp olive oil
225g/8oz fine green beans, trimmed
1 small cos or romaine lettuce or 2 Little
   Gem (Bibb) lettuces
4 new potatoes, boiled
4 tomatoes, or 12 cherry tomatoes
2 red (bell) peppers, seeded and cut into
   thin strips
4 hard-boiled eggs
8 drained anchovy fillets in oil, halved
   lengthways
16 large black olives
salt and ground black pepper
12 fresh basil leaves, to garnish

FOR THE DRESSING
15ml/1 tbsp red wine vinegar
90ml/6 tbsp olive oil
1 fat garlic clove, crushed

1 Brush the tuna on both sides with a little olive oil and season with salt and pepper. Heat a ridged griddle pan or the grill (broiler) until very hot, then cook the tuna steaks for 1–2 minutes on each side; the flesh should still be pink and juicy in the middle. Set aside.

2 Cook the beans for 4 minutes. Drain, refresh under cold water and drain again.

3 Arrange the lettuce leaves on four serving plates. Slice the potatoes and tomatoes, if large, and divide them among the plates. Arrange the fine green beans and red pepper strips over them.

4 Shell the eggs and cut them into halves. Place two half eggs on each plate with an anchovy fillet draped over. Sprinkle four olives on to each plate.

5 To make the dressing, whisk together the vinegar, olive oil and garlic and seasoning to taste. Drizzle over the salads, arrange the tuna steaks on top, sprinkle over the basil and serve.

Nutritional information per portion: Energy 578kcal/2408kJ; Protein 46.4g; Carbohydrate 15g, of which sugars 10.6g; Fat 37.5g, of which saturates 7.1g; Cholesterol 235mg; Calcium 127mg; Fibre 4.7g; Sodium 585mg.

Provençal aioli with salt cod

This substantial salad is one of the nicest dishes for summer entertaining. Vary the vegetables according to what is in season; include radishes, yellow pepper and celery for colour contrast.

SERVES 6

1kg/2¹/₄ lb salt cod, soaked overnight in water to cover
1 fresh bouquet garni
18 small new potatoes, scrubbed
1 large fresh mint sprig, torn
225g/8oz green beans, trimmed
225g/8oz broccoli florets
6 hard-boiled eggs
12 baby carrots, with leaves if possible, scrubbed
1 large red (bell) pepper, seeded and cut into strips
2 fennel bulbs, cut into strips
18 red or yellow cherry tomatoes
6 large whole cooked prawns (shrimp) in the shell, to garnish (optional)

FOR THE AIOLI

600ml/1 pint/2¹/₂ cups mayonnaise
2 fat garlic cloves, crushed
cayenne pepper

1 Drain the cod and put it into a shallow pan. Pour in barely enough water to cover the fish and add the bouquet garni. Bring to the boil, then cover and poach very gently for about 10 minutes, until the fish flakes easily when tested with the tip of a sharp knife. Drain and set aside until required.

2 Cook the potatoes with the mint in a pan of lightly salted, boiling water until just tender. Drain and set aside. Cook the beans and broccoli in separate pans of lightly salted, boiling water for about 3–5 minutes. They should still be very crisp. Refresh under cold water and drain again, then set aside.

3 Remove the skin from the cod and break the flesh into large flakes. Shell and halve the eggs lengthways.

4 Pile the cod on a serving platter and arrange the eggs and the vegetables around it. Garnish with the prawns if you are using them.

5 To make the aioli, put the mayonnaise in a bowl and add the garlic and cayenne pepper to taste. Serve in individual bowls or one large bowl.

Energy 1099kcal/4567kJ; Protein 66.5g; Carbohydrate 21.4g, of which sugars 10.2g; Fat 83.9g, of which saturates 13.6g; Cholesterol 364mg; Calcium 140mg; Fibre 5.6g; Sodium 1217mg.

Herring and potato salad

This is the perfect main dish for a hot summer's day. A firm yellow waxy potato variety is best for this salad, which includes flavoursome herrings presented on round lettuce.

SERVES 2

6–8 waxy potatoes

1 round (butterhead) lettuce, coarse outer leaves removed

2 hard-boiled eggs, halved

100g/3¾oz extra-mature (sharp) Gouda cheese, cut into thin strips

4 marinated herrings, drained

2 spring onions (scallions), chopped

4 large sweet pickled gherkins, sliced

45ml/3 tbsp olive oil

15ml/1 tbsp white wine vinegar

salt and ground black pepper

chopped fresh parsley, to garnish

50g/2oz/¼ cup butter, melted, and mustard, oil and vinegar, to serve

1 Scrape the potatoes, remove the 'eyes' and cook in plenty of boiling water for about 20 minutes, until they are tender. Drain well and keep warm.

2 Tear the lettuce into bitesize pieces and spread out on a serving platter. Arrange the egg halves and strips of cheese on top.

3 Cut the herrings into small pieces and add to the platter.

4 Sprinkle the herrings with the spring onions and gherkins.

5 Whisk together the oil and vinegar in a bowl, season with salt and pepper and sprinkle the dressing over the salad. Garnish with chopped parsley.

6 Serve with the potatoes and a sauceboat of the melted butter, with mustard, oil and vinegar added to taste.

Nutritional information per portion: Energy 862kcal/3577kJ; Protein 38g; Carbohydrate 21g, of which sugars 13.5g; Fat 69.8g, of which saturates 27.3g; Cholesterol 328mg; Calcium 477mg; Fibre 1.9g; Sodium 1525mg.

Herring salad

The Dutch love matjes herring, a special kind of tender herring that is produced by gutting and salting the fish at sea immediately after they have been caught.

SERVES 4

1 lettuce, finely shredded
1 shallot, finely chopped
15ml/1 tbsp chopped fresh dill
15ml/1 tbsp vegetable oil
15ml/1 tbsp white wine vinegar
2 eating apples
2 cooked beetroots (beets)
2 boiled potatoes (optional)
15ml/1 tbsp cocktail onions
15ml/1 tbsp coarsely chopped gherkins, plus 30ml/2 tbsp of the vinegar from the jar
2–4 hard-boiled eggs
4 matjes herrings, with skin and backbones removed
salt and ground black pepper
chopped fresh chives, to garnish

1 Mix together the lettuce, shallot, dill, oil and vinegar in a bowl and season with salt and pepper. Spread out on a flat platter.

2 Peel, core and dice the apples, then peel and dice the beetroots and potatoes, if using.

3 Mix together the apples, beetroots, potatoes, if using, cocktail onions, gherkins and vinegar from the jar in another bowl. Then spoon the mixture into the middle of the platter.

4 Mash the eggs with a fork. Make a border of mashed egg around the platter. Garnish with the chives.

5 Cut off and discard the tails of the herrings and halve the fish. Curl the halved fish over the middle of the dish and serve.

Nutritional information per portion: Energy 315kcal/1323kJ; Protein 21.4g; Carbohydrate 19.5g, of which sugars 18.8g; Fat 17g, of which saturates 1.2g; Cholesterol 137mg; Calcium 58mg; Fibre 2.3g; Sodium 901mg.

Smoked fish salad

Smoked oily fish – salmon, eels, sprats, perch, trout and herring – are well suited to this recipe. These rich fish are complemented by sharp dressings and pungent, relish-type sauces, such as this simple yet delicious version, made with horseradish and mustard.

SERVES 4

500g/1¼lb smoked eel fillet
5ml/1 tsp Swedish or German mustard
5ml/1 tsp grated fresh horseradish
about 50ml/2fl oz/¼ cup double
    (heavy) cream
4 smoked sprats, skinned and filleted
ground black pepper
a handful of mixed lettuce leaves and boiled
    new potatoes, to serve

FOR THE DRESSING

100ml/3½fl oz/scant ½ cup double
    (heavy) cream
5ml/1 tsp mustard
5ml/1 tsp grated fresh horseradish
a little lemon juice

1 Remove the skin from the smoked eel by peeling it off with your fingers, much as you would skin a banana. Place the skinned, smoked eel on a board and cut about half of it into four neat fillets. Set aside.

2 Put the remaining smoked eel fillet in a food processor, add the mustard and horseradish and season with pepper. Blend until smooth, adding enough cream to form a firm paste.

3 Spoon a dollop of the smoked eel paste on to a bed of lettuce on four individual serving plates.

4 Carefully remove the skin from the smoked sprats using a small, sharp knife, then arrange the skinned fish around the paste, together with the reserved smoked eel fillets.

5 To make the dressing, whisk together the cream, mustard, horseradish and a few drops of lemon juice, until stiff. Spoon on to the salad and serve with boiled new potatoes.

Nutritional information per portion: Energy 487kcal/2021kJ; Protein 30.8g; Carbohydrate 0.9g, of which sugars 0.7g; Fat 40.2g, of which saturates 17.3g; Cholesterol 285mg; Calcium 94mg; Fibre 0g; Sodium 257mg.

Asparagus and smoked fish salad

A mixture of white and green asparagus is served with a green sauce. The recipe includes seven different fresh herbs; if you can't find them all, use larger amounts of any that you have.

SERVES 4

600g/1lb 6oz white asparagus, peeled and
cut diagonally into 1cm/1/2in pieces
300g/11oz green asparagus, peeled and
sliced as above
20ml/4 tsp sunflower oil
1 onion, finely sliced
15ml/1 tbsp cider vinegar
15ml/1 tbsp apple juice
10 cherry tomatoes, halved
400g/14oz mixed smoked fish (salmon,
trout, eel, mackerel or halibut)
salt, ground white pepper and sugar
finely chopped parsley, to garnish

FOR THE GREEN SAUCE

200ml/7fl oz/scant 1 cup natural
(plain) yogurt
200ml/7fl oz/scant 1 cup sour cream
5ml/1 tsp medium-hot mustard
juice of 1/2 lemon
2 hard-boiled eggs, separated into yolk and
white
10ml/2 tsp sunflower oil
150g/5oz fresh herbs (chervil, parsley,
chives, watercress, sorrel, borage and
salad burnet), very finely chopped

1 Cook the asparagus in separate pans in salted water for 4–5 minutes. Drain and refresh under cold water. Put the white asparagus in a bowl and set the green aside.

2 Fry the onion over medium heat for 2 minutes. Add the vinegar and apple juice. Season with salt, pepper and sugar. Bring the mixture to the boil and remove from the heat. Pour the dressing over the white asparagus. Stir in the cherry tomatoes and marinate the salad for 1–2 hours.

3 To make the green sauce, mix the yogurt, sour cream, mustard and lemon juice. Season to taste with salt, pepper and sugar. Mash the egg yolk and blend with the oil. Stir into the yogurt and cream mixture. Dice the egg white and add to the dressing, with the chopped herbs.

4 Drain the asparagus and tomatoes from the dressing and toss with the green asparagus and chopped parsley. Arrange the salad on serving plates, with the fish. Serve the sauce on the side.

Nutritional information per portion: Energy 644kcal/2664kJ; Protein 34.2g; Carbohydrate 13.4g, of which sugars 12.5g; Fat 50.9g, of which saturates 14.4g; Cholesterol 230mg; Calcium 319mg; Fibre 6.1g; Sodium 864mg.

Smoked fish and horseradish sauce

This combination of cold horseradish sauce and smoked fish has been a Dutch classic since 1795. Smoked eel is the most popular choice for this dish, but you can substitute any other smoked fish.

SERVES 4

300g/11oz smoked trout, cut into strips
150g/5oz lamb's lettuce
60ml/4 tbsp cress
2 radishes, sliced
30ml/2 tbsp very finely chopped
   fresh parsley
50g/2oz/½ cup cooked brown prawns
   (shrimp) or other small prawns
8 canned anchovy fillets, drained
15ml/1 tbsp grated horseradish
30ml/2 tbsp mayonnaise
salt and ground black pepper
lemon wedges, to garnish
toasted white bread and butter, to serve

1 Place the smoked trout in a small dish, add water to cover and soak for 30 minutes. Drain and pat dry with kitchen paper.

2 Divide the lamb's lettuce among four plates. Arrange the cress around the edges of the plates and add the radishes. Place the trout strips in the lamb's lettuce and surround with a ring of parsley and a ring of prawns.

3 Top each plate with two anchovy fillets and garnish with lemon wedges.

4 Mix together the horseradish and mayonnaise in a bowl and season to taste with salt and pepper.

5 Serve the smoked fish with the horseradish sauce and with toast and butter.

Nutritional information per portion: Energy 134kcal/561kJ; Protein 19.5g; Carbohydrate 3.1g, of which sugars 2.7g; Fat 4.9g, of which saturates 0.3g; Cholesterol 30mg; Calcium 89mg; Fibre 1.4g; Sodium 413mg.

Smoked trout and noodle salad

It is important to use ripe juicy tomatoes for this fresh-tasting salad. For a special occasion you could replace the smoked trout with smoked salmon.

SERVES 4

225g/8oz somen noodles
2 smoked trout, skinned and boned
2 hard-boiled eggs, coarsely chopped
30ml/2 tbsp chopped fresh chives,
    to garnish
lime halves, to serve (optional)

FOR THE DRESSING

6 ripe plum tomatoes, cored and chopped
2 shallots, finely chopped
30ml/2 tbsp tiny capers, rinsed
30ml/2 tbsp chopped fresh tarragon
finely grated rind and juice of 1/2 orange
60ml/4 tbsp extra virgin olive oil
salt and ground black pepper

1 To make the dressing, place the tomatoes in a bowl with the shallots, capers, tarragon, orange rind, orange juice and olive oil. Season with salt and ground black pepper, and mix well. Leave the dressing to marinate at room temperature for 1–2 hours.

2 Cook the noodles in a large pan of boiling water until just tender. Drain and rinse under cold running water. Drain again well.

3 Toss the noodles with the tomato and onion dressing, then add salt and ground black pepper to taste. Arrange the noodles on a large serving platter or individual plates.

4 Flake the smoked trout over the noodles, then sprinkle the coarsely chopped eggs and chopped chives over the top. Serve the lime halves on the side, if you like.

Nutritional information per portion: Energy 474kcal/1979kJ; Protein 26g; Carbohydrate 51.5g, of which sugars 5.3g; Fat 17.6g, of which saturates 3.1g; Cholesterol 121mg; Calcium 49mg; Fibre 1.5g; Sodium 1464mg.

Smoked trout pasta salad

The fennel and dill really complement the flavour of the smoked trout in this delicious dish and the little pasta shells catch the trout, creating tasty mouthfuls.

SERVES 8

15g/¹/₂oz/1 tbsp butter
175g/6oz/1 cup chopped fennel bulb
6 spring onions (scallions), 2 finely
    chopped and the rest thinly sliced
225g/8oz skinless smoked trout
    fillets, flaked
45ml/3 tbsp chopped fresh dill

120ml/4fl oz/¹/₂ cup mayonnaise
10ml/2 tsp fresh lemon juice
30ml/2 tbsp whipping cream
450g/1lb/4 cups small pasta shapes, such
    as conchiglie
salt and ground black pepper
dill sprigs, to garnish

1 Melt the butter in a small pan. Cook the fennel and minced spring onions for 3–5 minutes. Transfer to a large bowl and cool slightly.

2 Add the sliced spring onions, trout, dill, mayonnaise, lemon juice and cream. Season and mix.

3 Bring a large pan of water to the boil. Salt to taste and add the pasta. Cook according to the instructions on the packet until just al dente. Drain thoroughly and leave to cool.

4 Add the pasta to the vegetable and trout mixture and toss to coat evenly. Check seasoning and add salt and ground black pepper, if necessary. Serve the salad lightly chilled or at room temperature, garnished with sprigs of dill.

Nutritional information per portion: Energy 369kcal/1548kJ; Protein 14.5g; Carbohydrate 42.7g, of which sugars 2.8g; Fat 16.8g, of which saturates 4g; Cholesterol 29mg; Calcium 31mg; Fibre 2.3g; Sodium 613mg.

Shellfish Salads

This section presents a selection of shellfish prepared in many different ways from a variety of cuisines. There are mussels, prawns, squid, clams, crabs, whelks, octopus and scallops mingling with herbs, spices, salad leaves, vegetables and grains. Some salads are simply dressed, such as Crab Salad with Coriander, or there are more exotic flavours in Seafood Salad with Fragrant Herbs or Piquant Prawn Salad.

Potato, mussel and watercress salad

This is a speciality of Galicia in north-west Spain, where they claim that the mussels found on the Atlantic coast are the best in the world. They are also very proud of their potatoes and watercress. A creamy, well-flavoured dressing enhances all these ingredients.

SERVES 4

675g/1½lb salad potatoes
1kg/2¼lb fresh mussels, scrubbed and
   beards removed
200ml/7fl oz/scant 1 cup dry white wine
15g/½oz fresh flat leaf parsley, chopped
a bunch of watercress or rocket (arugula)
salt and ground black pepper
chopped fresh chives, to garnish

FOR THE DRESSING

105ml/7 tbsp olive oil
15–30ml/1–2 tbsp white wine vinegar
5ml/1 tsp strong Dijon mustard
1 large shallot, very finely chopped
15ml/1 tbsp chopped fresh chives
45ml/3 tbsp double (heavy) cream
pinch of caster (superfine)
   sugar (optional)

1 Cook the potatoes in salted, boiling water for 15–20 minutes, or until tender. Drain, cool, then peel. Slice the potatoes into a bowl and toss with 30ml/2 tbsp of the oil for the dressing.

2 Discard any open mussels that do not close when sharply tapped. Bring the white wine to the boil in a large, heavy pan. Add the mussels, cover and boil vigorously, shaking the pan occasionally, for 3–4 minutes, until the mussels have opened. Discard any that do not open. Drain and shell the mussels, reserving the cooking liquid. Boil the liquid until reduced to about 45ml/3 tbsp. Strain this through a fine sieve (strainer) over the potatoes and mix.

3 Make the dressing. Whisk together the remaining oil, 15ml/1 tbsp of the vinegar, the mustard, shallot and chives. Add the cream and whisk again until thick. Add more vinegar and/or a pinch of sugar to taste.

4 Toss the mussels and potatoes with the dressing and parsley. Arrange the watercress or rocket and salad on a platter. Sprinkle with chives.

Nutritional information per portion: Energy 459kcal/1918kJ; Protein 17.2g; Carbohydrate 29.2g, of which sugars 3.8g; Fat 27.7g, of which saturates 7g; Cholesterol 45mg; Calcium 222mg; Fibre 2.5g; Sodium 231mg.

Seafood salad

This is a very pretty and appetizing arrangement of fresh mussels, prawns and squid rings served on a colourful bed of salad vegetables. In Spain, where the dish comes from, canned albacore tuna is also often included in this type of simple salad.

SERVES 6

115g/4oz prepared squid rings
12 fresh mussels, scrubbed and bearded
1 large carrot
6 crisp lettuce leaves
10cm/4in piece cucumber, finely diced
115g/4oz cooked, peeled prawns (shrimp)
15ml/1 tbsp drained pickled capers

FOR THE DRESSING
30ml/2 tbsp lemon juice
45ml/3 tbsp virgin olive oil
15ml/1 tbsp chopped fresh parsley
salt and ground black pepper

1 Put the squid rings into a metal sieve (strainer) or steamer. Place the sieve or steamer over a pan of simmering water, cover with a lid and steam the squid for 2–3 minutes, until it just turns white. Cool under cold running water to prevent further cooking and drain thoroughly on kitchen paper.

2 Discard any open mussels that do not close when tapped. Cover the base of a large pan with water, add the mussels, then cover and steam for a few minutes until they open. Discard any that remain shut.

3 Using a swivel-style vegetable peeler, cut the carrot into wafer-thin ribbons. Tear the lettuce into pieces and arrange on a serving plate. Sprinkle the carrot ribbons on top, then sprinkle over the diced cucumber.

4 Arrange the mussels, prawns and squid rings over the salad and sprinkle the capers over the top.

5 Make the dressing. Put all the ingredients in a small bowl and whisk well to combine. Drizzle over the salad. Serve at room temperature.

Nutritional information per portion: Energy 294kcal/1235kJ; Protein 17.3g; Carbohydrate 22.4g, of which sugars 1.4g; Fat 12.8g, of which saturates 1.9g; Cholesterol 132mg; Calcium 99mg; Fibre 1.3g; Sodium 140mg.

Insalata di mare

You can vary the fish in this Italian salad according to what is available, but try to include at least two kinds of shellfish and some squid. The salad is good warm or cold.

**SERVES 6 AS AN APPETIZER,
4 AS A MAIN COURSE**

450g/1lb fresh mussels, scrubbed and
　bearded
450g/1lb small clams, scrubbed
105ml/7 tbsp dry white wine
225g/8oz squid, cleaned
4 large scallops, with their corals
30ml/2 tbsp olive oil
2 garlic cloves, finely chopped
1 small dried red chilli, crumbled
225g/8oz whole cooked prawns (shrimp), in
　the shell

6–8 large chicory (Belgian endive) leaves
6–8 radicchio leaves
15ml/1 tbsp chopped flat leaf parsley, to
　garnish

FOR THE DRESSING
5ml/1 tsp Dijon mustard
30ml/2 tbsp white wine vinegar
5ml/1 tsp lemon juice
120ml/4fl oz/$\frac{1}{2}$ cup extra virgin olive oil
salt and ground black pepper

1 Discard any dead mussels and clams; put the remainder in a pan with the wine. Cover and cook over a high heat, shaking now and then, for 4 minutes, until they have opened. Discard any that remain closed. Transfer the shellfish to a bowl, strain and reserve the cooking liquid and set it aside.

2 Cut the squid into thin rings; chop the tentacles. Halve the scallops. Heat the oil and sauté the garlic, chilli, squid, scallops and corals for 2 minutes. Lift the squid and scallops out of the pan and leave to cool; reserve the oil.

3 Remove the shells, keeping a dozen of each in the shell. Peel all but 6–8 of the prawns. Pour the shellfish cooking liquid into a pan, set over a high heat and reduce by half. Mix all the shelled and unshelled mussels and clams with the squid and scallops, then add the prawns.

4 To make the dressing, whisk the mustard with the vinegar and lemon juice and season. Whisk in the olive oil, the reserved cooking liquid and the oil from the frying pan. Add the dressing to the shellfish mixture and toss. Arrange the chicory and radicchio leaves on a serving dish and pile the mixed shellfish salad into the centre. Sprinkle with the parsley and serve.

Nutritional information per portion: Energy 445kcal/1861kJ; Protein 41.1g; Carbohydrate 3.7g, of which sugars 1g; Fat 27.9g, of which saturates 4.3g; Cholesterol 241mg; Calcium 219mg; Fibre 0.5g; Sodium 585mg.

Crab salad with rocket

If the dressed crabs are really small, you could pile the salad back into the shells for an alternative presentation, and serve as an appetizer.

SERVES 4

white and brown meat from 4 small fresh
  dressed crabs, about 450g/1lb
1 small red (bell) pepper, seeded and
  finely chopped
1 small red onion, finely chopped
30ml/2 tbsp drained capers
30ml/2 tbsp chopped fresh coriander
  (cilantro)
grated rind and juice of 2 lemons
a few drops of Tabasco sauce
40g/1½ oz rocket (arugula) leaves
30ml/2 tbsp sunflower oil
15ml/1 tbsp fresh lime juice
salt and ground black pepper
lemon rind strips, to garnish

1 Put the white and brown crab meat, red pepper, onion, capers and chopped coriander in a bowl. Add the grated lemon rind and juice and toss gently to mix together. Season with a few drops of Tabasco sauce, according to taste, then add a little salt and ground black pepper to taste.

2 Wash the rocket leaves and thoroughly pat dry on kitchen towels. Divide the rocket between four individual plates.Whisk together the oil and lime juice in a small bowl. Dress the rocket leaves, then carefully pile the crab salad on top and serve garnished with lemon rind strips.

Nutritional information per portion: Energy 164kcal/686kJ; Protein 21.4g; Carbohydrate 4.3g, of which sugars 3.8g; Fat 6.9g, of which saturates 0.8g; Cholesterol 81mg; Calcium 167mg; Fibre 1.5g; Sodium 625mg

Crab salad with coriander

Crab has sweet succulent meat and is full of flavour. In this recipe, the white and brown crabmeat are mixed together and simply dressed with a tasty, creamy sauce, then served in a salad.

SERVES 2

1 head romaine lettuce
2 eating apples
juice of 1 lemon
a bunch of spring onions (scallions),
**   chopped**
150ml/¹⁄₄ pint/²⁄₃ cup whipping cream
135ml/4¹⁄₂ fl oz crème fraîche
30ml/2 tbsp chopped fresh coriander
**   (cilantro), plus extra to garnish**
brown and white meat of 2 crabs
salt

1 Arrange the lettuce leaves in a shallow side dish.

2 Peel, quarter and core the apples then cut into small dice. Put in a bowl, add the lemon juice and toss together. Add the spring onions and mix together.

3 Whisk the cream in a large bowl until it stands in soft peaks, then fold in the crème fraîche. Add the apple mixture and the coriander.

4 Mix together the brown and white crab meat and season with a little salt to taste.

5 Fold the crab meat into the cream mixture. Check the seasoning and arrange the crab meat over the lettuce leaves.

6 Serve the salad immediately, garnished with the chopped coriander.

Nutritional information per portion: Energy 382kcal/1585kJ; Protein 20.6g; Carbohydrate 6.4g, of which sugars 6.2g; Fat 30.6g, of which saturates 19.3g; Cholesterol 151mg; Calcium 188mg; Fibre 1.4g; Sodium 571mg.

Seafood salad in mustard dressing

The classic Korean ingredients of seafood, chestnuts and salad vegetables are given a new twist here with the addition of English mustard, giving the dish a pleasant heat. Simple to prepare, this is a perfect quick snack or appetizer.

SERVES 2

50g/2oz squid, prepared
50g/2oz king prawns (jumbo shrimp)
50g/2oz cooked whelks
90g/3½oz Asian pear
⅓ carrot
½ medium cucumber
25g/1oz Chinese leaves (Chinese cabbage), shredded
25g/1oz chestnuts, cooked, peeled and sliced
25g/1oz crab meat or seafood stick

FOR THE DRESSING

15ml/1 tbsp ready-made English (hot) mustard
30ml/2 tbsp sugar
15ml/1 tbsp full cream (whole) milk
45ml/3 tbsp cider vinegar
5ml/1 tsp chilli oil
2.5ml/½ tsp dark soy sauce
5ml/1 tsp salt

1 Rinse the pouch and tentacles of the squid well. Score the squid with a crisscross pattern, and slice into strips about 2cm/½in wide.

2 Hold each prawn between two fingers and pull off the tail shell. Twist off the head. Peel away the soft body shell and the small claws. Make a shallow cut down the centre of the curved back of the prawn. Pull out the black vein with a cocktail stick (toothpick). Rinse well. Slice the prawns into similar sized pieces.

3 Bring a pan of lightly salted water to the boil and cook the squid and prawns for 3 minutes, then drain. Thinly slice the whelks. Peel the Asian pear and cut the pear and the carrot into thin strips. Seed the cucumber and cut into thin strips.

4 Combine all the dressing ingredients in a bowl until they are well blended. Arrange the vegetable strips on a large serving platter with the Chinese leaves and chestnuts. Arrange the seafood on the platter, including the crab meat or seafood stick. Pour over the dressing and chill well in the refrigerator before serving.

Nutritional information per portion: Energy 206kcal/872kJ; Protein 18g; Carbohydrate 29.8g, of which sugars 23.9g; Fat 2.4g, of which saturates 0.6g; Cholesterol 230mg; Calcium 62mg; Fibre 2.4g; Sodium 1282mg.

Crab meat salad with garlic dressing

The combination of Asian pear and pineapple juice makes a light, refreshing complement to the sweetness of the crab in this recipe. A zesty dressing with mustard creates a balance of flavours and sliced cucumber adds a welcome texture.

SERVES 2–3

45ml/3 tbsp sugar
30ml/2 tbsp cider vinegar
30ml/2 tbsp pineapple juice
5ml/1 tsp grated fresh root ginger
1 Asian pear, cored and finely sliced
1 cucumber, peeled, seeded and
   finely sliced
10ml/2 tsp cornflour (cornstarch)
150g/5oz raw crab meat
20g/³⁄₄oz cress, to garnish

FOR THE DRESSING

30ml/2 tbsp Dijon mustard
30ml/2 tbsp white wine vinegar
2 garlic cloves, crushed
15ml/1 tbsp pineapple juice
5ml/1 tsp dark soy sauce
5ml/1 tsp salt
30ml/2 tbsp sugar

1 Combine the sugar, cider vinegar, pineapple juice and ginger in a bowl. Add 1.5 litres/2½ pints/6¼ cups chilled water and stir gently until the sugar has dissolved. Add the Asian pear and cucumber and leave for 10 minutes, then drain and set aside.

2 Place the cornflour in a heatproof bowl that will fit in a steamer and add the crab meat. Mix together gently to coat the crab meat evenly.

3 Place a steamer over a pan of boiling water and put the bowl of crab meat inside it. Cover and steam for 10 minutes and then set the crab to one side to cool.

4 For the dressing, combine the mustard, vinegar, garlic, pineapple juice, soy sauce, salt and sugar, then stir in 50ml/2fl oz water.

5 Place the pear, cucumber and crab meat in a serving dish and pour over the dressing. Toss the salad and garnish with cress before serving.

Nutritional information per portion: Energy 149kcal/630kJ; Protein 10.8g; Carbohydrate 21.2g, of which sugars 17.9g; Fat 2.9g, of which saturates 0.4g; Cholesterol 36mg; Calcium 34mg; Fibre 0.5g; Sodium 812mg.

Octopus salad

Choose young small specimens of octopus because they will be much more tender and require less cooking time. Octopus is eaten in many countries but this recipe, which includes olives, oil and vinegar, is popular around the Adriatic Sea.

SERVES 4–6

900g/2lb baby octopus or squid, skinned
175ml/6fl oz/³⁄₄ cup olive oil
30ml/2 tbsp white wine vinegar
30ml/2 tbsp chopped fresh parsley
     or coriander (cilantro)
12 black olives, pitted
2 shallots, thinly sliced
1 red onion, thinly sliced
salt and freshly ground black pepper
sprigs of coriander (cilantro), to garnish
8–12 cos or romaine lettuce leaves and
     lemon wedges, to serve

1 In a large pan, boil the octopus or squid in salted water for 20–25 minutes, or until just soft. Strain and leave to cool before covering and chilling for 45 minutes.

2 Cut the tentacles from the body and head, then chop all the flesh into even pieces, slicing across the thick part of the tentacles following the direction of the suckers.

3 In a bowl, combine the olive oil and white wine vinegar.

4 Add the parsley or coriander, olives, shallots, octopus and red onion to the bowl. Season to taste and toss well.

5 Arrange the octopus on a bed of lettuce, garnish with coriander and serve with lemon wedges.

Nutritional information per portion: Energy 199kcal/834kJ; Protein 30g; Carbohydrate 0.5g, of which sugars 0.3g; Fat 8.6g, of which saturates 1.4g; Cholesterol 80mg; Calcium 60mg; Fibre 0.2g; Sodium 1mg.

Genoese squid salad

This colourful Italian-style salad is popular for summer days, when green beans and new potatoes are in peak condition. It makes a perfect lunch dish.

SERVES 4–6

450g/1lb prepared squid, cut into rings
4 garlic cloves, roughly chopped
300ml/½ pint/1¼ cups Italian red wine
450g/1lb waxy new potatoes, scrubbed
225g/8oz green beans, trimmed and cut
    into short lengths
2–3 sun-dried tomatoes in oil, drained
    and thinly sliced lengthwise
60ml/4 tbsp extra virgin olive oil
15ml/1 tbsp red wine vinegar
salt and ground black pepper

1 Preheat the oven to 180°C/350°F/Gas 4. Put the squid rings in an ovenproof dish with half the garlic, the wine and pepper to taste. Cover and cook for 45 minutes, or until the squid is tender.

2 Meanwhile, put the potatoes in a pan, cover with cold water and add a good pinch of salt. Bring to the boil, cover and simmer for about 15 minutes, until tender. Using a slotted spoon, lift out the potatoes and set aside. Add the beans to the boiling water and cook for 3 minutes. Drain.

3 When the potatoes are cool enough to handle, slice them thickly on the diagonal and place them in a bowl with the warm beans and sun-dried tomatoes. Whisk the oil, vinegar and the remaining garlic in a bowl and add salt and pepper to taste. Pour over the potato mixture.

4 Drain the squid and discard the liquid. Add the squid to the potato mixture and mix very gently. Arrange on individual plates and season liberally with pepper before serving.

Nutritional information per portion: Energy 239kcal/999kJ; Protein 13.6g; Carbohydrate 14.3g, of which sugars 1.9g; Fat 10.9g, of which saturates 1.7g; Cholesterol 169mg; Calcium 31mg; Fibre 1.6g; Sodium 94mg.

Squid and seaweed with chilli dressing

This chilled seafood salad has delicious flavours of chilli and rice vinegar that are balanced by sweet maple syrup, with the kelp providing an unusual and tantalizing aroma and taste.

SERVES 2

400g/14oz squid, prepared
200g/7oz dried kelp
2 cucumbers, thinly sliced
10ml/2 tsp sesame seeds
6 spring onions (scallions), finely chopped
2 dried red chillies, finely chopped
salt

FOR THE DRESSING

30ml/2 tbsp rice vinegar
2 garlic cloves, crushed
60ml/4 tbsp gochujang chilli paste
60ml/4 tbsp maple syrup
15ml/1 tsp grated fresh root ginger

1 Rinse the pouch and tentacles of the squid well. Use a sharp knife to score the squid with a crisscross pattern, and slice into generous pieces about 4cm/1½ in long.

2 Soak the kelp in cold water for 20 minutes and blanch in boiling water for 1 minute, draining it almost immediately to retain its texture and colour. Squeeze any excess water from the leaves by hand. Roughly chop the kelp into bitesize pieces.

3 Put the cucumber in a colander and sprinkle with salt. Leave to stand for 10 minutes, then pour away any excess liquid. Put the dressing ingredients in a large bowl and mix together till blended.

4 Bring a pan of water to the boil. Add the squid and simmer for 3 minutes, stirring, then drain under cold running water.

5 Put the squid, cucumber and kelp on a platter and add the dressing. Chill and sprinkle with the sesame seeds, spring onions and chillies before serving.

Nutritional information per portion: Energy 321kcal/1354kJ; Protein 35.6g; Carbohydrate 30g, of which sugars 27.3g; Fat 7.3g, of which saturates 1.3g; Cholesterol 450mg; Calcium 247mg; Fibre 3.3g; Sodium 433mg.

Seafood and asparagus salad

This crustacean salad originates on the west coast of Sweden, which abounds with fresh seafood. The salad has become a stylish classic in that country where it is traditionally served with cold beer.

SERVES 6–8

200g/7oz fresh asparagus spears
1kg/2¼lb shell-on cooked prawns (shrimp)
200g/7oz can mussels in brine
100g/3½oz can crab meat in brine or the
   meat from 2 large cooked crabs
200g/7oz small mushrooms, sliced
1 cos or romaine lettuce, finely chopped

FOR THE DRESSING
105ml/7 tbsp mayonnaise
5ml/1 tsp tomato purée (paste)

pinch of salt
1 garlic clove, crushed
15ml/1 tbsp chopped fresh dill

FOR THE GARNISH
1 potato
vegetable oil, for deep-frying
4 baby tomatoes, quartered
2 lemons, cut into wedges
1 bunch fresh dill

1 Stand the asparagus spears upright in a deep pan or put in an asparagus pan, pour in enough boiling water to come three-quarters of the way up the stalks and simmer for about 10 minutes until tender. Drain and, when cool enough to handle, cut into 5cm/2in lengths.

2 Carefully remove the shells from the prawns, keeping them intact. Drain the brine from the mussels, and the crab if using canned, then carefully mix the prawns with the mussels, crab meat, asparagus and mushrooms.

3 To make the potato garnish, very finely grate the potato and rinse under cold running water to wash off the starch. Put the potato on a clean dish towel and pat dry. Heat the oil in a deep-fryer or pan to 180–190°C/ 350–375°F or until a cube of bread browns in 30 seconds. Add the potato and fry until golden brown then remove from the pan with a slotted spoon. Drain on kitchen paper and leave to cool.

4 To make the dressing, mix the mayonnaise, tomato purée, salt, garlic and dill. Add the dressing to the fish mixture and mix carefully. To serve, arrange the chopped lettuce on individual plates. Place the salad on the lettuce and garnish with the fried potato, tomatoes, lemon wedges and dill.

Nutritional information per portion: Energy 594kcal/2531kJ; Protein 113.3g; Carbohydrate 2.8g, of which sugars 1.2g; Fat 14.6g, of which saturates 2.9g; Cholesterol 1337mg; Calcium 565mg; Fibre 0.9g; Sodium 7723mg.

Seafood salad with fragrant herbs

This is a spectacular salad made with cellophane noodles. The luscious combination of prawns, scallops and squid makes it the ideal choice for a special celebration.

SERVES 4–6

250ml/8fl oz/1 cup fish stock or water
350g/12oz squid, cleaned and cut into rings
12 raw king prawns (jumbo shrimp), peeled, with tails intact
12 scallops
50g/2oz cellophane noodles, soaked in warm water for 30 minutes
1/2 cucumber, cut into thin batons
1 lemon grass stalk, finely chopped
2 kaffir lime leaves, finely shredded
2 shallots, thinly sliced

30ml/2 tbsp chopped spring onions (scallions)
30ml/2 tbsp fresh coriander (cilantro) leaves
12–15 fresh mint leaves, coarsely torn
4 fresh red chillies, seeded and cut into slivers
juice of 1–2 limes
30ml/2 tbsp Thai fish sauce
fresh coriander (cilantro) sprigs, to garnish

1 Pour the fish stock or water into a medium pan, set over a high heat and bring to the boil. Cook each type of seafood separately in the stock for 3–4 minutes. Remove with a slotted spoon and set aside to cool.

2 Drain the noodles. Using scissors, cut them into short lengths, about 5cm/2in long. Place them in a serving bowl and add the cucumber, lemon grass, kaffir lime leaves, shallots, spring onions, coriander, mint and chillies.

3 Pour over the lime juice and fish sauce. Mix well, then add the seafood. Toss lightly. Garnish with the fresh coriander sprigs and serve.

Nutritional information per portion: Energy 135kcal/568kJ; Protein 22.3g; Carbohydrate 4.6g, of which sugars 4.3g; Fat 3.1g, of which saturates 0.5g; Cholesterol 100mg; Calcium 173mg; Fibre 1.5g; Sodium 359mg.

Rice salad with shrimp

In this versatile Thai recipe, use whatever fruit, vegetables and even leftover meat that you might have, just mix with cooked rice and pour over the fragrant dressing.

SERVES 4–6

350g/12oz/3 cups cooked rice

1 Asian pear, cored and diced

50g/2oz dried shrimp, chopped

1 avocado, peeled, stoned (pitted) and diced

½ medium cucumber, finely diced

2 lemon grass stalks, finely chopped

30ml/2 tbsp sweet chilli sauce

1 fresh green or red chilli, seeded and
    finely sliced

115g/4oz/1 cup flaked (sliced)
    almonds, toasted

a small bunch of fresh coriander
    (cilantro), chopped

fresh Thai sweet basil leaves, to garnish

FOR THE DRESSING

300ml/ ½ pint/1 ¼ cups water

10ml/2 tsp shrimp paste

15ml/1 tbsp palm sugar (jaggery) or light
    muscovado (brown) sugar

2 kaffir lime leaves, torn into small pieces

½ lemon grass stalk, sliced

1 Make the dressing. Put the measured water in a small pan with the shrimp paste, sugar, kaffir lime leaves and lemon grass. Heat gently, stirring, until the sugar dissolves, then bring to boiling point and simmer for 5 minutes. Strain into a bowl and set aside until cold.

2 Put the cooked rice in a large salad bowl and fluff up the grains with a fork. Add the Asian pear, dried shrimp, avocado, cucumber, lemon grass and sweet chilli sauce. Mix well.

3 Add the sliced chilli, almonds and coriander to the bowl and toss well. Garnish with Thai basil leaves and serve with the bowl of dressing to spoon over the top of individual portions.

Nutritional information per portion: Energy 398kcal/1664kJ; Protein 16.2g; Carbohydrate 34.9g, of which sugars 6.7g; Fat 22.4g, of which saturates 2.6g; Cholesterol 63mg; Calcium 249mg; Fibre 4.1g; Sodium 550mg.

Piquant prawn salad

A Thai-inspired dressing adds a superb flavour to the noodles and prawns in this delicious recipe. The salad can be served warm or cold, and will serve six as an appetizer.

SERVES 4

200g/7oz rice vermicelli
8 baby corn cobs, halved
150g/5oz mangetouts (snow peas)
15ml/1 tbsp vegetable oil
2 garlic cloves, finely chopped
2.5cm/1in piece fresh root ginger, peeled
    and finely chopped
1 fresh red or green chilli, seeded and
    finely chopped
450g/1lb raw peeled tiger prawns
    (jumbo shrimp)
4 spring onions (scallions), thinly sliced
15ml/1 tbsp sesame seeds, toasted
1 lemon grass stalk, thinly shredded,
    to garnish

FOR THE DRESSING

15ml/1 tbsp chopped fresh chives
15ml/1 tbsp Thai fish sauce
5ml/1 tsp soy sauce
45ml/3 tbsp groundnut (peanut) oil
5ml/1 tsp sesame oil
30ml/2 tbsp rice vinegar

1 Put the rice vermicelli in a wide heatproof bowl, pour over boiling water and leave for 5 minutes. Drain, refresh under cold water and drain well again. Return to the bowl and set aside until required.

2 Boil or steam the corn cobs and mangetouts for about 3 minutes; they should still be crunchy. Refresh under cold water and drain. Now make the dressing. Mix all the ingredients for the dressing in a screw-top jar, close tightly and shake well to combine.

3 Heat the oil in a large frying pan or wok. Add the garlic, ginger and red or green chilli and cook for 1 minute. Add the tiger prawns and stir-fry for about 3 minutes, until they have just turned pink. Stir in the spring onions, corn cobs, mangetouts and sesame seeds, and toss lightly to mix.

4 Pour the mixture over the rice vermicelli. Pour the dressing on top and toss well. Serve, garnished with lemon grass, or chill for an hour before serving.

Nutritional information per portion: Energy 216kcal/906kJ; Protein 17.6g; Carbohydrate 27.4g, of which sugars 1.1g; Fat 4g, of which saturates 0.6g; Cholesterol 146mg; Calcium 97mg; Fibre 0.9g; Sodium 147mg.

Banana blossom salad with prawns

Banana blossom doesn't actually taste of banana. Instead it is mildly tannic, similar to an unripe persimmon – a taste and texture that complements chillies, lime and fish sauce.

SERVES 4

2 banana blossom hearts
juice of 1 lemon
225g/8oz cooked peeled prawns (shrimp)
30ml/2 tbsp roasted peanuts, finely chopped, fresh basil leaves and lime slices, to garnish

FOR THE DRESSING

juice of 1 lime
30ml/2 tbsp white rice vinegar
60ml/4 tbsp nuoc mam or fish sauce
45ml/3 tbsp palm sugar (jaggery) or light muscavado (brown) sugar
3 red Thai chillies, seeded and finely sliced

1 Cut the banana blossom hearts into quarters lengthwise and then slice them very finely crossways. To prevent them discolouring, put the slices in a bowl of cold water mixed with the lemon juice and leave to soak for about 30 minutes.

2 To make the dressing, beat the lime juice, vinegar, and nuoc mam or tuk trey with the sugar in a small bowl, until it has dissolved. Stir in the chillies and garlic and set aside.

3 Drain the sliced banana blossom and put it in a serving bowl. Add the prawns and pour over the dressing. Toss well to coat the banana blossom and prawns.

4 Garnish with the roasted peanuts, basil leaves and lime slices.

Nutritional information per portion: Energy 103kcal/438kJ; Protein 11g; Carbohydrate 15g. of which sugars 13g; fat 0.5g, of which saturates 0.1g; Cholesterol 110mg; Calcium 54mg; fibre 0.7g; Sodium 109mg

Prawn noodle salad with fragrant herbs

This light salad combines all the tangy flavours of the sea. Instead of prawns, you could also use any other shellfish, such as squid, scallops, clams, mussels or crab meat.

SERVES 4

1/2 cucumber
115g/4oz cellophane noodles
1 small green (bell) pepper, seeded and
    cut into strips
1 tomato, cut into strips
2 shallots, finely sliced
16 cooked peeled prawns (shrimp)
salt and ground black pepper
fresh coriander (cilantro) leaves,
    to garnish

FOR THE DRESSING
15ml/1 tbsp rice wine vinegar
30ml/2 tbsp Thai fish sauce
30ml/2 tbsp lime juice
2.5ml/ 1/2 tsp grated fresh root ginger
1 lemon grass stalk, finely chopped
1 fresh red chilli, seeded and finely sliced
30ml/2 tbsp roughly chopped fresh mint
few sprigs of tarragon, roughly chopped
15ml/1 tbsp chopped fresh chives
pinch of salt

1 To make the dressing, combine all the ingredients in a small bowl and whisk well.

2 Soak the noodles in hot water for 15–30 minutes until soft. Peel the cucumber, then scoop out the seeds and cut the flesh into batons.

3 Drain the noodles, then plunge them in a pan of boiling water for 1 minute. Drain, rinse under cold running water and drain again well.

4 In a large bowl, combine the noodles with the green pepper, cucumber, tomato and shallots. Lightly season with salt and pepper, then toss with the dressing.

5 Spoon the noodles on to individual serving plates, arranging the prawns on top. Garnish with a few coriander leaves and serve immediately.

Nutritional information per portion: Energy 156kcal/653kJ; Protein 7.4g; Carbohydrate 29.4g, of which sugars 5.4g; Fat 0.7g, of which saturates 0.1g; Cholesterol 49mg; Calcium 68mg; Fibre 2.1g; Sodium 417mg

Thai prawn salad with garlic dressing and frizzled shallots

In this intensely flavoured salad, juicy prawns and sweet mango are partnered with a sweet-and-sour garlic dressing which is heightened with the hot taste of chilli. The crispy frizzled shallots are a traditional addition to Thai salads.

SERVES 4–6

675g/1¹/₂lb medium raw prawns (shrimp), peeled and deveined, with tails intact
finely shredded rind of 1 lime
¹/₂ fresh red chilli, seeded and finely chopped
30ml/2 tbsp olive oil, plus extra for brushing
1 ripe but firm mango
2 carrots, cut into long thin shreds
10cm/4in piece cucumber, sliced
1 small red onion, halved and thinly sliced
45ml/3 tbsp roasted peanuts, coarsely chopped

4 large shallots, thinly sliced and fried until crisp in 30ml/2 tbsp groundnut (peanut) oil
salt and ground black pepper

FOR THE DRESSING
1 large garlic clove, chopped
10–15ml/2–3 tsp caster (superfine) sugar
juice of 2 limes
15–30ml/1–2 tbsp Thai fish sauce
1 fresh red chilli, seeded and finely chopped
5–10ml/1–2 tsp light rice vinegar

1 Place the prawns in a non-metallic dish with the lime rind, chilli, oil and seasoning. Toss to mix thoroughly and leave to marinate at room temperature for 30–40 minutes.

2 Make the dressing. Place the garlic in a mortar with 10ml/2 tsp of the caster sugar. Pound with a pestle until smooth, then work in about three-quarters of the lime juice, followed by 15ml/1 tbsp of the Thai fish sauce.

3 Transfer the dressing to a jug (pitcher). Stir in half the chopped red chilli. Taste the dressing and add more sugar, lime juice and/or fish sauce, if you think they are necessary, and stir in light rice vinegar to taste.

4 Peel and stone (pit) the mango. The best way to do this is to cut either side of the large central stone (pit), as close to it as possible, with a sharp knife. Cut the flesh into very fine strips and cut off any flesh still adhering to the stone.

5 Place the mango in a bowl and add the carrots, cucumber and red onion. Pour over about half the dressing and toss thoroughly. Arrange the salad on four to six individual plates or bowls.

6 Heat a ridged, cast-iron griddle pan or heavy frying pan until very hot. Brush with a little oil, then sear the marinated prawns for 2–3 minutes on each side, until they turn pink and are patched with brown on the outside. Arrange the prawns on the salads.

7 Sprinkle the remaining dressing over the salads. Sprinkle over the remaining chilli with the peanuts and crisp-fried shallots. Serve immediately.

Nutritional information per portion: Energy 292kcal/1222kJ; Protein 33.5g; Carbohydrate 13.4g, of which sugars 11.8g; Fat 11.9g, of which saturates 2g; Cholesterol 329mg; Calcium 160mg; Fibre 2.7g; Sodium 596mg.

Pomelo salad

This Thai salad, which features tropical fruit, is healthy and refreshing, and bursting with a mixture of assertive but complementary flavours.

SERVES 4–6

30ml/2 tbsp vegetable oil
4 shallots, finely sliced
2 garlic cloves, finely sliced
1 large pomelo
15ml/1 tbsp roasted peanuts
115g/4oz cooked peeled prawns (shrimp)
115g/4oz cooked crab meat
10–12 small fresh mint leaves

FOR THE DRESSING
30ml/2 tbsp Thai fish sauce
15ml/1 tbsp palm sugar (jaggery) or
    light muscovado (brown) sugar
30ml/2 tbsp fresh lime juice

FOR THE GARNISH
2 spring onions (scallions), thinly sliced
2 fresh red chillies, seeded and thinly sliced
fresh coriander (cilantro) leaves
shredded fresh coconut (optional)

1 To make the dressing, mix the fish sauce, sugar and lime juice together. Whisk well, then cover with clear film (plastic wrap) and set aside.

2 Heat the oil in a small frying pan, add the shallots and garlic and cook over a medium heat until they are golden. Remove from the pan and set aside.

3 Peel the pomelo and break into small pieces, removing membranes.

4 Grind the peanuts coarsely and put in a bowl. Add the pomelo, prawns, crab meat, mint and shallot mixture. Pour over the dressing, toss and sprinkle with the spring onions, chillies and coriander and shredded coconut, if using. Serve immediately.

Nutritional information per portion: Energy 159kcal/665kJ; Protein 13.4g; Carbohydrate 8.4g, of which sugars 8.1g; Fat 8.2g, of which saturates 1.1g; Cholesterol 44mg; Calcium 107mg; Fibre 1.1g; Sodium 1004mg.

Seafood salad with fruity dressing

Here, white fish is briefly seared, then served with prawns and salad tossed in an oil-free apricot and apple dressing. The fruit flavours make a delicate accompaniment to the fish.

SERVES 4

1 baby onion, sliced lengthways
lemon juice
400g/14oz very fresh sea bream or sea
    bass, filleted
30ml/2 tbsp sake
4 large king prawns (jumbo shrimp),
    heads and shells removed
about 400g/14oz mixed salad leaves

FOR THE DRESSING

2 ripe apricots, skinned and
    stoned (pitted)
1/4 eating apple, peeled and cored
60ml/4 tbsp second dashi stock or the
    same amount of water and 5ml/1 tsp
    dashi-no-moto
10ml/2 tsp shoyu
salt and ground white pepper

1 Soak the onion in ice-cold water for 30 minutes. Drain. Bring a pan half-full of water to the boil. Add a dash of lemon juice and plunge the fish into it. Remove the fish after 30 seconds and cool under cold running water. Cut into 8mm/1/3in thick slices crossways.

2 Bring the sake to the boil, then add the king prawns. Cook for 1 minute, or until they turn pink.

3 Cool the prawns under cold running water and cut into 1cm/1/2in thick slices crossways.

4 Slice an apricot thinly and set aside. Purée the remaining dressing ingredients. Chill. Lay out some salad leaves on plates. Mix the fish, prawns, apricot and onion together, add the remaining leaves, then toss with the dressing. Serve at once, on top of the salad leaves.

Nutritional information per portion: Energy 157kcal/662kJ; Protein 25g; Carbohydrate 5.3g, of which sugars 4.9g; Fat 3.2g, of which saturates 0.5g; Cholesterol 129mg; Calcium 186mg; Fibre 1.6g; Sodium 299mg.

Asparagus and langoustine salad

For a really extravagant treat, you could make this attractive salad with medallions of lobster. For a cheaper version, use large prawns (shrimp), allowing six per serving.

SERVES 4

16 langoustines
16 fresh asparagus spears, trimmed
2 carrots
30ml/2 tbsp olive oil
1 garlic clove, peeled
15ml/1 tbsp chopped fresh tarragon
4 fresh tarragon sprigs and some chopped, to
   garnish

FOR THE DRESSING
30ml/2 tbsp tarragon vinegar
120ml/4fl oz/¹/₂ cup olive oil
salt and ground black pepper

1 Shell the langoustines and keep the discarded parts for stock. Set aside.

2 Steam the asparagus over salted, boiling water until just tender, but still a little crisp. Refresh under cold water, drain and place in a shallow dish.

3 Peel the carrots and cut into fine julienne shreds. Cook in a pan of salted, boiling water for about 3 minutes, until tender but still crunchy. Drain, refresh under cold water and drain again. Place in the dish with the asparagus.

4 Make the dressing. Whisk the vinegar with the oil in a jug (pitcher). Season to taste. Pour over the asparagus and carrots and leave to marinate.

5 Heat the oil with the garlic in a frying pan until very hot. Add the langoustines and sauté quickly until just heated through. Discard the garlic.

6 Cut the asparagus spears in half and arrange on four individual plates with the carrots. Drizzle over the dressing left in the dish and top each portion with four langoustine tails. Add the tarragon sprigs and sprinkle with the chopped tarragon. Serve.

Nutritional information per portion: Energy 320kcal/1323kJ; Protein 16.3g; Carbohydrate 4g, of which sugars 3.8g; Fat 26.6g, of which saturates 3.9g; Cholesterol 146mg; Calcium 93mg; Fibre 2.3g; Sodium 150mg.

Poultry Salads

Chicken and duck are universally popular and versatile meats that are deliciously light and refreshing in salads. Thai Chicken Salad is a renowned recipe from Chiang Mai that is delightfully tasty at any time, and Warm Chicken Salad with Hazelnut Dressing makes a simple and quick lunch or supper dish. Duck gets a zesty Asian treatment in Shredded Duck and Bean Thread Noodle Salad, which is perfect for a light meal.

Tangy chicken salad

This fresh and lively dish typifies the character of Thai cuisine. It is ideal for a light lunch on a hot and lazy summer's day. The creamy coconut dressing is the perfect contrast to the spicy chilli.

SERVES 4–6

4 skinless, boneless chicken breasts

2 garlic cloves, crushed

30ml/2 tbsp soy sauce

30ml/2 tbsp vegetable oil

115g/4oz/½ cup water chestnuts, sliced

50g/2oz/½ cup cashew nuts, roasted
   and coarsely chopped

4 shallots, thinly sliced

4 kaffir lime leaves, thinly sliced

1 lemon grass stalk, thinly sliced

5ml/1 tsp chopped fresh galangal

1 large fresh red chilli, seeded and
   finely chopped

2 spring onions (scallions), thinly sliced

10–12 fresh mint leaves, torn

1 lettuce, roughly sliced

2 fresh red chillies, seeded
   and sliced, to garnish

FOR THE DRESSING

120ml/4fl oz/½ cup coconut cream

30ml/2 tbsp Thai fish sauce

juice of 1 lime

30ml/2 tbsp palm sugar (jaggery) or
   light muscovado (brown) sugar

1 Place the chicken in a large dish. Rub with the garlic, soy sauce and 15ml/1 tbsp of the oil. Cover and leave to marinate for 1–2 hours.

2 Heat the remaining oil in a wok or frying pan. Stir-fry the chicken for 3–4 minutes on each side, or until cooked. Set aside to cool.

3 In a pan, heat the coconut cream, fish sauce, lime juice and sugar. Stir until the sugar dissolves; set aside.

4 Tear the cooked chicken breasts into strips and put them in a bowl. Add the water chestnuts, cashew nuts, shallots, kaffir lime leaves, lemon grass, galangal, chopped red chilli, spring onions and mint leaves to the chicken.

5 Pour the coconut dressing over the mixture and toss well. Arrange the lettuce on serving plates, place the salad on top and garnish with the sliced red chillies.

Nutritional information per portion: Energy 404kcal/1691kJ; Protein 40.4g; Carbohydrate 11.3g, of which sugars 9g; Fat 22.3g, of which saturates 9.8g; Cholesterol 105mg; Calcium 25mg; Fibre 0.8g; Sodium 666mg.

Coronation chicken

Originally devised as part of the feast to celebrate the coronation of Elizabeth II in 1953, this chicken salad has been appearing on buffet tables countrywide ever since.

SERVES 8

1/2 lemon
2.25kg/5lb chicken
1 onion, quartered
1 carrot, quartered
1 large bouquet garni
8 black peppercorns, crushed
salt and ground black pepper
watercress or parsley sprigs, to garnish

FOR THE SAUCE

1 small onion, chopped
15g/1/2 oz/1 tbsp butter
15ml/1 tbsp curry paste
15ml/1 tbsp tomato purée (paste)
125ml/4fl oz/1/2 cup red wine
1 bay leaf
juice of 1/2 lemon, or to taste
10–15ml/2–3 tsp apricot jam
300ml/1/2 pint/11/4 cups mayonnaise
125ml/4fl oz/1/2 cup whipping cream

1 Put the lemon half in the chicken cavity, then place it in a close-fitting pan. Add the vegetables, bouquet garni, peppercorns and a little salt.

2 Add water to come two-thirds of the way up the chicken, bring just to the boil, cover and cook very gently for 11/2 hours, until the chicken juices run clear. Leave to cool.

3 When the chicken is cold remove the skin and bones and chop the flesh.

4 To make the sauce, cook the onion in the butter until soft. Add the curry paste, tomato purée, wine, bay leaf and lemon juice, then cook for 10 minutes. Add the jam, press through a sieve (strainer) and cool.

5 Beat the mayonnaise into the sauce. Whip the cream and gently fold it in; add seasoning and lemon juice, then stir in the chicken. Garnish with watercress or parsley and serve.

Nutritional information per portion: Energy 587kcal/2429kJ; Protein 10.1g; Carbohydrate 17.1g, of which sugars 4.7g; Fat 51.6g, of which saturates 8.8g; Cholesterol 228mg; Calcium 97mg; Fibre 1.1g; Sodium 401mg.

Chicken, vegetable and chilli salad

A great way to use up leftover chicken, this spicy salad is full of surprising textures and flavours. Serve as a light lunch dish or for supper with rice or noodles.

SERVES 4

225g/8oz Chinese leaves (Chinese cabbage)
2 carrots, cut into thin strips
1/2 cucumber, cut into thin strips
salt
2 fresh red chillies, seeded and cut into thin strips
1 small onion, sliced into fine rings
4 pickled gherkins, sliced, plus 45ml/3 tbsp of the liquid
50g/2oz/1/2 cup peanuts, coarsely ground
225g/8oz cooked chicken, finely sliced
1 garlic clove, crushed
5ml/1 tsp sugar
30ml/2 tbsp cider vinegar or white vinegar

1 Finely slice the Chinese leaves and set aside with the carrot strips. Spread out the cucumber strips on a board and sprinkle with salt. Set aside for 15 minutes.

2 Turn the salted cucumber into a colander, rinse well under cold running water and pat dry.

3 Mix together the chillies and onion rings and then add the sliced gherkins and peanuts.

4 Put the Chinese leaves in a salad bowl with the carrot and cucumber strips. Add the chilli and onion mixture and chicken.

5 Mix the gherkin liquid with the garlic, sugar and vinegar. Pour over the salad, toss lightly and serve immediately.

Nutritional information per portion: Energy 167kcal/700kJ; Protein 17.8g; Carbohydrate 9.1g, of which sugars 7.7g; Fat 6.9g, of which saturates 1.4g; Cholesterol 39mg; Calcium 47mg; Fibre 2.9g; Sodium 50mg.

Chicken and broccoli salad

Gorgonzola makes a tangy dressing that works perfectly with both chicken and broccoli. Serve for a lunch or supper dish with ciabatta.

SERVES 4

175g/6oz broccoli florets, divided into small sprigs

225g/8oz/2 cups dried farfalle pasta or other shapes

2 large cooked chicken breasts

FOR THE DRESSING

90g/3¹/₂oz Gorgonzola cheese

15ml/1 tbsp white wine vinegar

60ml/4 tbsp extra virgin olive oil

2.5–5ml/¹/₂–1 tsp finely chopped fresh sage, plus extra sage sprigs to garnish

salt and ground black pepper

1 Cook the broccoli florets in a large pan of salted boiling water for 3 minutes. Remove with a slotted spoon and rinse under cold running water, then spread out on kitchen paper to drain and dry.

2 Add the pasta to the broccoli cooking water, then bring back to the boil and cook according to the packet instructions. When cooked, drain the pasta, rinse under cold running water until cold, then leave to drain and dry.

3 Remove the skin from the cooked chicken breasts and cut the meat into bitesize pieces.

4 To make the dressing, mash the cheese with a fork in a large bowl, then whisk in the wine vinegar followed by the oil and sage and salt and pepper to taste. Add the pasta, chicken and broccoli to the dressing. Toss well, then adjust the seasoning and serve, garnished with sage.

Nutritional information per portion: Energy 472kcal/1977kJ; Protein 25.3g; Carbohydrate 42.5g, of which sugars 2.5g; Fat 23.5g, of which saturates 6.8g; Cholesterol 52mg; Calcium 151mg; Fibre 2.8g; Sodium 310mg.

Spicy Thai chicken salad

This spicy salad with flavours of Thailand is particularly good with roast chicken. It is simple and quick to make once the chicken has been cooked.

SERVES 4–6

450g/1lb chicken, cooked and shredded
1 head Chinese leaves (Chinese cabbage), shredded
2 carrots, finely grated (shredded)
a small bunch of fresh mint, chopped
a small bunch of fresh coriander (cilantro) leaves, to garnish

FOR THE DRESSING

30ml/2 tbsp groundnut (peanut) oil
30ml/2 tbsp white rice vinegar
45ml/3 tbsp Thai fish sauce
juice of 2 limes
30ml/2 tbsp palm sugar (jaggery) or light muscavado (brown) sugar
2 red Thai chillies, seeded and chopped
25g/1oz fresh young root ginger, sliced
3 garlic cloves, crushed
2 shallots, finely chopped

1 To make the dressing, beat the oil, vinegar, fish sauce and lime juice in a bowl with the sugar, until it has dissolved.

2 Stir in the red chillies, sliced ginger, garlic and shallots and leave to stand for about 30 minutes to allow the flavours to blend together and develop.

3 Put the cooked chicken strips, Chinese leaves, carrots and mint in a large bowl. Pour over the dressing and toss well together. Garnish with the fresh coriander leaves and serve.

COOK'S TIPS
• *If you want to use fresh chicken breast fillets in this recipe, slice the chicken finely, then stir-fry in a little oil heated in a wok or frying pan until cooked through.*
• *For a milder dressing, use fewer red Thai chillies, or substitute a milder chilli.*

Nutritional information per portion: Energy 156kcal/656kJ; Protein 20g; Carbohydrate 8.4g, of which sugars 7.9g; Fat 4.9g, of which saturates 0.7g; Cholesterol 53mg; Calcium 73mg; Fibre 3.1g; Sodium 596mg.

Egg noodle salad with sesame chicken

This quick and tasty salad is ideal for a midweek meal when you are short of time. You could use rice noodles, which would be even faster.

SERVES 4–6

400g/14oz fresh thin egg noodles
1 carrot, cut into long fine strips
50g/2oz mangetouts (snow peas), trimmed, shredded and blanched
115g/4oz/½ cup beansprouts, blanched
30ml/2 tbsp olive oil
225g/8oz skinless chicken breast fillet
30ml/2 tbsp sesame seeds, toasted
2 spring onions (scallions), sliced, and coriander (cilantro) leaves, to garnish

FOR THE DRESSING

45ml/3 tbsp sherry vinegar
75ml/5 tbsp soy sauce
60ml/4 tbsp sesame oil
90ml/6 tbsp light olive oil
1 garlic clove, finely chopped
5ml/1 tsp grated fresh root ginger
salt and ground black pepper

1 To make the dressing, whisk together all the ingredients in a small bowl, seasoning with salt and pepper to taste.

2 Cook the noodles in a large pan of boiling water according to the packet instructions. Be careful not to overcook them. Drain the noodles, rinse and drain well. Transfer to a bowl.

3 Add the carrot, mangetouts and beansprouts to the noodles. Pour in about half the dressing, then toss the mixture well and adjust the seasoning.

4 Heat the oil in a large frying pan. Finely slice the chicken, add to the pan and stir-fry for 3 minutes, or until cooked and golden. Remove from the heat. Add the sesame seeds and drizzle in some dressing.

5 Arrange the noodle mixture on individual plates, making a nest on each plate. Spoon the chicken on top. Sprinkle with the spring onions and coriander leaves and serve any remaining dressing separately.

Nutritional information per portion: Energy 546kcal/2286kJ; Protein 19.3g; Carbohydrate 50.9g, of which sugars 3.8g; Fat 30.9g, of which saturates 5.3g; Cholesterol 46mg; Calcium 69mg; Fibre 3.2g; Sodium 860mg.

Salmagundi

Elaborately arranged salads were fashionable in 16th-century England. They included chopped meat, anchovies and eggs, garnished with onions, lemon juice, oil and other condiments.

SERVES 4–6

1 large chicken, weighing about
 2kg/4¹/₂lb
1 onion
1 carrot
1 celery stick
2 bay leaves
large sprig of thyme
10 black peppercorns
500g/1¹/₄lb new or baby potatoes
225g/8oz carrots, cut into small sticks
225g/8oz sugar snap peas
4 eggs
¹/₂ cucumber, thinly sliced
8–12 cherry tomatoes
8–12 green olives stuffed with pimento

FOR THE DRESSING

75ml/5 tbsp olive oil
30ml/2 tbsp lemon juice
2.5ml/¹/₂ tsp sugar
1.5ml/¹/₄ tsp ready-made English (hot)
 mustard
salt and ground black pepper

1 Put the chicken in a deep pan with the onion, carrot, celery, bay leaves, thyme and peppercorns. Add water to cover by at least 2.5cm/1in. Bring to the boil and simmer gently for 45 minutes or until the chicken is cooked, then leave to cool in the stock for several hours to keep it moist.

2 In a bowl or jug (pitcher), whisk together the ingredients for the dressing. Set aside.

3 Using a separate pan for each, cook the potatoes, carrots and sugar snap peas in lightly salted boiling water until just tender. Drain and rinse under cold water. Halve the potatoes. Hard-boil the eggs, cool, shell and cut into quarters.

4 Lift the chicken out of the stock, remove the meat and cut or tear into bitesize pieces.

5 Arrange all the vegetables, the chicken and the eggs on a large platter, or in a large bowl, and add the tomatoes and olives. Just before serving, drizzle the salad dressing over the top.

Nutritional information per portion: Energy 397kcal/1664kJ; Protein 41.2g; Carbohydrate 24.9g, of which sugars 8.7g; Fat 15.5g, of which saturates 3g; Cholesterol 220mg; Calcium 63mg; Fibre 4.6g; Sodium 155mg.

Thai chicken salad

The city of Chiang Mai in the north-east of Thailand is famous for this chicken salad. It includes the typical Thai flavours of lime and lemon grass.

SERVES 4–6

450g/1lb minced (ground) chicken
1 lemon grass stalk, root trimmed
3 kaffir lime leaves, finely chopped
4 fresh red chillies, seeded and chopped
60ml/4 tbsp fresh lime juice
30ml/2 tbsp Thai fish sauce
15ml/1 tbsp roasted ground rice
2 spring onions (scallions), finely chopped
30ml/2 tbsp fresh coriander (cilantro)
  leaves
thinly sliced kaffir lime leaves, mixed
  salad leaves and fresh mint sprigs,
  to garnish

1 Heat a large, non-stick frying pan. Add the minced chicken and moisten with a little water. Stir constantly over a medium heat for 7–10 minutes, until cooked through.

2 Remove the pan from the heat and drain off any excess fat. Cut off the lower 5cm/2in of the lemon grass stalk and chop it finely.

3 Transfer the chicken to a bowl and add the chopped lemon grass, lime leaves, chillies, lime juice, fish sauce, roasted ground rice, spring onions and coriander. Mix well.

4 Spoon the chicken mixture into a salad bowl. Sprinkle sliced lime leaves over the top and garnish with salad leaves and sprigs of mint.

Nutritional information per portion: Energy 135kcal/572kJ; Protein 27.4g; Carbohydrate 3.4g, of which sugars 0.4g; Fat 1.3g, of which saturates 0.4g; Cholesterol 79mg; Calcium 8mg; Fibre 0.1g; Sodium 424mg.

Chicken and mango salad with orange rice

Contemporary British cooking is influenced by cuisines from all over the world. The way the chicken is spiced in this recipe derives inspiration from India.

SERVES 4

15ml/1 tbsp sunflower oil
1 onion, chopped
1 garlic clove, crushed
30ml/2 tbsp curry paste
10ml/2 tsp apricot jam
30ml/2 tbsp chicken stock
about 450g/1lb cooked chicken
150ml/¼ pint/⅔ cup natural (plain) yogurt
60–75ml/4–5 tbsp mayonnaise
1 large mango, cut into 1cm/½in dice
fresh flat leaf parsley sprigs, to garnish
poppadums, to serve

FOR THE ORANGE RICE

175g/6oz/scant 1 cup long grain rice
225g/8oz carrots, grated (about 1⅓ cups)
1 large orange, cut into segments
40g/1½oz/⅓ cup roasted flaked
    (sliced) almonds

FOR THE DRESSING

105ml/7 tbsp olive oil
45ml/3 tbsp lemon juice
1 garlic clove, crushed
15ml/1 tbsp chopped mixed fresh herbs
salt and ground black pepper

1 Heat the oil in a frying pan and fry the onion and garlic for 3–4 minutes until soft.

2 Stir in the curry paste, cook for about 1 minute, then lower the heat and stir in the apricot jam and stock. Cut the chicken into small pieces and add to the pan. Mix well and stir until the chicken is thoroughly coated in the paste. Spoon the mixture into a large bowl and leave to cool.

3 Meanwhile, boil the rice in plenty of lightly salted water until just tender. Drain, rinse under cold water and drain again. When cool, stir into the grated carrots and add the orange segments and flaked almonds. Mix together.

4 Make the dressing by whisking all the ingredients together in a bowl.

5 When the chicken mixture is cool, stir in the yogurt and mayonnaise, then add the mango and mix. Chill for about 30 minutes.

6 When ready to serve, pour the dressing into the rice salad and mix well. Spoon on to a platter and mound the cold curried chicken on top. Garnish with flat leaf parsley and serve with poppadums.

Nutritional information per portion: Energy 776kcal/3245kJ; Protein 35.9g; Carbohydrate 60.2g, of which sugars 21.1g; Fat 45.3g, of which saturates 6.4g; Cholesterol 93mg; Calcium 172mg; Fibre 4.5g; Sodium 206mg.

Orange chicken salad

With their tangy flavour, orange segments are the perfect partner for tender chicken in this tasty rice salad. To appreciate all the flavours fully, serve the salad at room temperature.

SERVES 4

3 large seedless oranges
175g/6oz/scant 1 cup long grain rice
175ml/6fl oz/³/₄ cup vinaigrette
10ml/2 tsp strong Dijon mustard
2.5ml/¹/₂ tsp caster (superfine) sugar
450g/1lb cooked chicken, diced
45ml/3 tbsp chopped fresh chives
75g/3oz/³/₄ cup almonds or cashew
   nuts, toasted
salt and ground black pepper
mixed salad leaves, to serve

1 Pare one of the oranges thinly, removing only the rind, not the pith. Put the pieces of orange rind in a pan and add the rice. Pour in 475ml/16fl oz/2 cups water, add a pinch of salt and bring to the boil. Cover and cook over a very low heat for 15 minutes, or until the rice is tender and the water has been absorbed.

2 Meanwhile, peel the oranges, removing all the pith. Separate them into segments over a plate. Add the orange juice from the plate to the

vinaigrette with the mustard and sugar, whisking to combine. Check the seasoning.

3 Discard the pieces of orange rind from the cooked rice. Spoon the rice into a bowl, let it cool slightly, then add half the dressing. Toss well, then set aside to cool completely.

4 Add the chicken, chives, nuts and orange segments to the rice. Pour over the remaining dressing and toss. Serve on a bed of salad leaves.

Nutritional information per portion: Energy 642kcal/2678kJ; Protein 35.6g; Carbohydrate 49.5g, of which sugars 14g; Fat 33.7g, of which saturates 4.7g; Cholesterol 79mg; Calcium 118mg; Fibre 3.5g; Sodium 278mg.

Citrus chicken salad

This zesty, refreshing salad is a good choice for a post-Christmas buffet, when cooked turkey can be used instead of chicken.

SERVES 6

120ml/4fl oz/½ cup extra virgin olive oil
6 boneless chicken breast
   portions, skinned
4 oranges
5ml/1 tsp Dijon mustard
15ml/1 tbsp clear honey
300g/11oz/2¾ cups white cabbage,
   finely shredded
300g/11oz carrots, finely sliced
2 spring onions (scallions), finely sliced
2 celery sticks, cut into matchsticks
30ml/2 tbsp chopped fresh tarragon
2 limes
salt and ground black pepper

1 Heat 30ml/2 tbsp of the oil in a large, heavy frying pan. Add the chicken breasts to the pan and cook for 15–20 minutes, or until the chicken is cooked through and golden brown. (If your pan is too small, cook the chicken in two or three batches.) Remove the chicken from the pan and leave to cool.

2 Peel two of the oranges, cutting off all pith, then cut out the segments from between the membranes and set aside. Grate the rind and squeeze the juice from one of the remaining oranges and place in a large bowl. Stir in the Dijon mustard, 5ml/1 tsp of the honey,

60ml/4 tbsp of the oil and seasoning to taste. Add the cabbage, carrots, spring onions and celery. Leave to stand for 10 minutes.

3 Meanwhile, squeeze the juice from the remaining orange and mix it with the remaining honey and oil, and the tarragon. Peel and segment the limes and lightly mix the segments into the dressing with the reserved orange segments. Season with salt and pepper to taste.

4 Slice the chicken breasts and stir into the citrus fruit. Spoon the vegetable salad on to plates and add the chicken mixture, then serve.

Nutritional information per portion: Energy 272kcal/1137kJ; Protein 25.7g; Carbohydrate 11.8g, of which sugars 11.7g; Fat 13.8g, of which saturates 2.1g; Cholesterol 70mg; Calcium 72mg; Fibre 2.6g; Sodium 71mg.

Warm chicken salad with hazelnut dressing

This simple warm salad combines pan-fried chicken and spinach with a light, fragrant, nutty dressing that includes a mixture of fresh herbs.

SERVES 4

45ml/3 tbsp olive oil

30ml/2 tbsp hazelnut oil

15ml/1 tbsp white wine vinegar

1 garlic clove, crushed

15ml/1 tbsp chopped fresh mixed herbs

225g/8oz baby spinach leaves

250g/9oz cherry tomatoes, halved

a bunch spring onions
    (scallions), chopped

2 skinless, boneless chicken breasts, cut
    into thin strips

salt and ground black pepper

1 First make the dressing. Place 30ml/2 tbsp of the olive oil, the hazelnut oil, vinegar, garlic and chopped herbs in a small bowl or jug (pitcher) and whisk together until well mixed. Set aside.

2 Trim any long stalks from the spinach leaves, then place in a large serving bowl with the tomatoes and spring onions and toss together to mix.

3 Heat the remaining 15ml/1 tbsp olive oil in a frying pan, add the chicken and stir-fry over a high heat for 7–10 minutes until the chicken is cooked and lightly browned.

4 Add the chicken to the salad, whisk the dressing, then drizzle it over the salad and gently toss all the ingredients together to mix. Season to taste with salt and pepper and serve immediately.

Nutritional information per portion: Energy 300kcals/1250kJ; Protein 23.2g; Carbohydrate 4.8g, of which sugars 4.5g; Fat 20.9g, of which saturates 2.7g; Cholesterol 21mg; Calcium 24mg; Fibre 2.4g; Sodium 126mg.

Israeli marinated chicken

Every street corner kiosk and stall in Israel seems to sell a version of this aromatic treat. The marinade is strongly scented with cumin and cinnamon.

SERVES 4

5 garlic cloves, chopped
30ml/2 tbsp ground cumin
7.5ml/1½ tsp ground cinnamon
5ml/1 tsp paprika
juice of 1 lemon
30ml/2 tbsp olive oil
1.3kg/3lb chicken, cut into 8 portions
salt and ground black pepper
fresh coriander (cilantro) leaves, to
　garnish
warmed pitta bread, chopped tomatoes,
　chopped cucumber, fresh chopped
　coriander and lemon wedges, to serve

1 In a bowl, combine the garlic, cumin, cinnamon, paprika, lemon juice, oil, salt and pepper. Add the chicken and turn to coat thoroughly. Leave to marinate for at least 1 hour or cover and place in the refrigerator overnight.

2 Light the barbecue. After about 40 minutes it will be ready for cooking.

3 Arrange the dark meat on the grill and cook for 10 minutes or until cooked through, turning once. Remove the meat once it is cooked and keep warm.

4 Place the remaining chicken on the grill and cook for 7–10 minutes, turning occasionally, until golden brown and the juices run clear when pricked with a skewer. Serve the chicken immediately, with pitta bread, tomatoes, cucumber, coriander and lemon wedges.

Nutritional information per portion: Energy 481kcal/1997kJ; Protein 40.8g; Carbohydrate 1g, of which sugars 0.1g; Fat 34.8g, of which saturates 8.9g; Cholesterol 215mg; Calcium 14mg; Fibre 0.3g; Sodium 147mg.

Chicken and pasta salad

Packed with colourful, crunchy veg and juicy chunks of cold roast chicken, this tasty salad is perfect for using up Sunday's leftover chicken.

SERVES 4

salt, a pinch of salt
350g/12oz short pasta, such as mezze
 rigatoni, fusilli or penne
45ml/3 tbsp olive oil
225g/8oz cold cooked chicken
2 small red or yellow peppers
4 spring onions, 4
50g/2oz/1/3 cup pitted green olives
45ml/3 tbsp mayonnaise
5ml/1 tsp Worcestershire sauce
15ml/1 tbsp wine vinegar,
salt and ground black pepper
a few fresh basil leaves, to garnish

1 Add water to a large pan until it is two-thirds full. Add a pinch of salt then bring to the boil. Add the pasta and bring back to the boil. Cook for 8–10 minutes, or according to packet instructions, until just tender (al dente). Drain and rinse, then put in a bowl. Toss with the olive oil.

2 Meanwhile, cut the chicken into bitesize pieces using a knife. Remove any bones, skin or fat. Add to the bowl.

3 Cut the peppers in half and remove the seeds and the membranes; discard.

4 Chop the peppers into bitesize pieces. Trim the spring onions and slice.

5 Add, along with all the remaining ingredients to the bowl, season and mix. Garnish with basil to serve.

Nutritional information per portion: Energy 65kcal/273kJ; Protein 2.6g; Carbohydrate 13.3g, of which sugars 7.6g; Fat 0.6g, of which saturates 0.1g; Cholesterol 0mg; Calcium 11mg; Fibre 0.4g; Sodium 171mg.

Korean chicken salad

Hot, spicy, garlicky and with a touch of sweetness, the chicken is perfectly tempered by the mild lettuce leaves in this attractive salad.

SERVES 4

900g/2lb chicken breast fillet or
    boneless thighs
2 round (butterhead) lettuces
vegetable oil
4 spring onions (scallions), shredded

FOR THE MARINADE
60ml/4 tsp gochujang chilli paste
45ml/3 tbsp mirin or rice wine
15ml/1 tbsp dark soy sauce
4 garlic cloves, crushed
25ml/5 tsp sesame oil
15ml/1 tbsp grated fresh root ginger
2 spring onions (scallions), finely chopped
10ml/2 tsp ground black pepper
15ml/1 tbsp lemonade

1 Combine all the marinade ingredients in a large bowl.

2 Cut the chosen chicken into bitesize pieces, add to the bowl and stir to coat it with the marinade. Transfer to an airtight container and marinate in the refrigerator for about 3 hours.

3 Remove the outer leaves from the heads of lettuce, keeping them whole. Rinse well, drain, and place on a serving dish.

4 Lightly coat a heavy griddle pan or frying pan with vegetable oil and place it over a medium heat (the griddle can also be used over a barbecue. Griddle or fry the chicken for 15 minutes, or until the meat is cooked and is a deep brown colour. Increase the heat briefly to scorch the chicken and give it a smoky flavour.

5 Serve by wrapping the chicken pieces in lettuce leaves with a few shredded spring onions.

Nutritional information per portion: Energy 279kcal/1178kJ; Protein 55g; Carbohydrate 2g, of which sugars 2g; Fat 5.7g, of which saturates 1.1g; Cholesterol 158mg; Calcium 39mg; Fibre 0.9g; Sodium 405mg.

Spiced quail with mixed leaf and mushroom salad

This is a perfect supper dish for autumnal entertaining. Quail is at its best when the breast meat is removed from the carcass, so that it cooks quickly.

SERVES 4

8 quail breasts
50g/2oz/¼ cup butter
5ml/1 tsp paprika
salt and ground black pepper

FOR THE SALAD
60ml/4 tbsp walnut oil
30ml/2 tbsp olive oil
45ml/3 tbsp balsamic vinegar
25g/1oz/2 tbsp butter
75g/3oz/generous 1 cup chanterelle mushrooms, sliced, if large
25g/1oz/3 tbsp walnut halves, toasted
115g/4oz mixed salad leaves

1 Preheat the grill (broiler). Arrange the quail breasts on the grill rack, skin side up. Dot with half the butter and sprinkle with half the paprika and a little salt.

2 Grill (broil) the quail breasts for 3 minutes, then turn them over and dot with the remaining butter, then sprinkle with the remaining paprika and a little salt. Grill for a further 3 minutes, or until they are cooked through. Transfer the quail breasts to a warmed dish, cover and leave to stand while preparing the salad.

3 Make the dressing first. Whisk the oils with the balsamic vinegar, then season and set aside. Heat the butter until foaming and cook the chanterelles for about 3 minutes, or until just beginning to soften. Add the walnuts and heat through. Remove from the heat.

4 Thinly slice the cooked quail breasts and arrange them on four individual serving plates with the warmed chanterelle mushrooms and walnuts and mixed salad leaves. Drizzle the oil and vinegar dressing over the salad and serve warm.

Nutritional information per portion: Energy 443kcal/1837kJ; Protein 25.6g; Carbohydrate 0.9g, of which sugars 0.8g; Fat 37.5g, of which saturates 12.3g; Cholesterol 110mg; Calcium 24mg; Fibre 0.7g; Sodium 176mg.

Indonesian chicken and prawn salad

Spicy and rich, chicken and shellfish salads are popular at Indonesian food stalls and as part of large, celebratory feasts. This classic dish is spiced with the sweet, gingery heat of galangal.

SERVES 4

500g/1¼lb chicken breast fillets
225g/8oz prawns (shrimp), shelled
30ml/2 tbsp groundnut (peanut) oil
5ml/1 tsp terasi (Indonesian
    shrimp paste)
10ml/2 tsp sugar
2 tomatoes, skinned, seeded and chopped
1 bunch fresh coriander (cilantro) leaves
1 bunch fresh mint leaves, chopped
juice of 1 lime
salt and ground black pepper
1 lime, quartered, and 2 red chillies,
    to garnish

FOR THE SPICE PASTE

2 shallots, chopped
2 garlic cloves, chopped
2–3 red chillies, seeded and chopped
25g/1oz galangal, chopped
2.5ml/½ tsp ground turmeric
1 lemon grass stalk, chopped

1 Cook the chicken pieces by steaming, roasting or boiling. When cooked, cut the meat into thin strips. Set aside.

2 Boil or steam the prawns for 2–3 minutes until pink and tender, drain and refresh under cold running water then drain again. Set aside.

3 To make the spice paste, using a mortar and pestle, grind the shallots, garlic, chillies, galangal, turmeric and lemon grass together.

4 Heat the oil in a heavy pan, stir in the spice paste and fry until fragrant. Add the terasi and palm sugar and stir for 3–4 minutes, until it begins to brown. Chop the coriander, then add the tomatoes, coriander, mint and lime juice to the pan and cook for 5–10 minutes, until the sauce is reduced and thick. Season to taste and turn into a large bowl. Leave to cool.

5 Add the chicken and prawns to the bowl and toss together. Transfer to a serving dish and serve garnished with the lime wedges and the chillies.

Nutritional information per portion: Energy 274kcal/1154kJ; Protein 41.6g; Carbohydrate 10.4g, of which sugars 8.7g; Fat 7.7g, of which saturates 1.1g; Cholesterol 197mg; Calcium 99mg; Fibre 2.2g; Sodium 193mg.

Roast chicken with cucumber and tomato salad

Cucumber and tomato salads are so simple yet versatile. Add them to mezze spreads for their refreshing flavour and crunchy texture; or tuck into pitta and flat bread wraps for a snack.

SERVES 6

1 small cucumber, peeled and diced
3 tomatoes, peeled, seeded and chopped
2 spring onions (scallions), chopped
30ml/2 tbsp olive oil
a small bunch of flat leaf parsley,
    finely chopped
a small bunch of mint, finely chopped
1/2 preserved lemon, finely chopped
45–60ml/3–4 tbsp tahini
juice of 1 lemon
2 garlic cloves, crushed
6 pitta breads
1/2 small roast chicken or 2 large roast
    chicken breasts, cut into strips
salt and ground black pepper

1 Place the cucumber in a colander over a bowl, sprinkle with a little salt and leave for 10 minutes to drain. Rinse well and drain again, then place in a bowl with the tomatoes and spring onions. Stir in the olive oil, parsley, mint and preserved lemon. Season well.

2 In a small bowl, mix the tahini with the lemon juice, then thin the mixture down with a little water to the consistency of thick double (heavy) cream. Beat in the garlic and season.

3 Preheat the grill (broiler) to hot. Lightly toast the pitta breads well away from the heat source until they puff up. (Alternatively, lightly toast the breads in a toaster.) Open the breads and stuff them liberally with the chicken and salad. Drizzle a generous amount of tahini sauce into each one and serve immediately.

Nutritional information per portion: Energy 300kcal/1259kJ; Protein 18.3g; Carbohydrate 31.4g, of which sugars 3.6g; Fat 12.1g, of which saturates 2g; Cholesterol 22mg; Calcium 146mg; Fibre 3.1g; Sodium 307mg.

Shredded duck and bean thread noodle salad

This refreshing, piquant salad makes a mouthwatering first course or light meal. The rich flavour of duck is offset by the addition of fresh, raw vegetables and zesty dressing.

SERVES 4

4 duck breast portions
30ml/2 tbsp Chinese rice wine
10ml/2 tsp finely grated fresh root ginger
60ml/4 tbsp soy sauce
15ml/1 tbsp sesame oil
15ml/1 tbsp clear honey
10ml/2 tsp Chinese five-spice powder
toasted sesame seeds, to sprinkle

FOR THE NOODLES

150g/5oz bean-thread noodles
a small handful of fresh mint leaves
a few coriander (cilantro) leaves
1 red (bell) pepper, seeded and sliced
4 spring onions (scallions), shredded
50g/2oz mixed salad leaves

FOR THE DRESSING

45ml/3 tbsp light soy sauce
30ml/2 tbsp mirin
10ml/2 tsp caster (superfine) sugar
1 garlic clove, crushed
10ml/2 tsp chilli oil

1 Place the duck breast portions in a bowl. Mix the rice wine, ginger, soy sauce, sesame oil, clear honey and five-spice powder. Toss to coat, cover and marinate in the refrigerator for 3–4 hours.

2 Transfer the duck and marinade to a large sheet of double thickness of foil on a heatproof plate. Enclose the duck and juices and seal the edges.

3 Place a steamer rack in a large wok and add 5cm/2in water. Bring to the boil and lower the plate on to it. Cover tightly, reduce the heat and steam for 50–60 minutes. Remove from the wok and leave to rest for 15 minutes.

4 Meanwhile, place the noodles in a large bowl and cover with boiling water. Cover and soak for 5–6 minutes. Drain, refresh under cold water and drain again. Transfer to a bowl with the herbs, red pepper, spring onions and leaves.

5 Mix the dressing ingredients. Skin the duck and shred the flesh. Divide the salad and duck among four plates. Add the dressing and sesame seeds and serve.

Nutritional information per portion: Energy 398kcal/1671kJ; Protein 32.8g; Carbohydrate 41.7g, of which sugars 10.8g; Fat 11.6g, of which saturates 2.2g; Cholesterol 165mg; Calcium 40mg; Fibre 1g; Sodium 1688mg.

Sesame duck and noodle salad

This salad is complete in itself and makes a satisfying summer lunch. The blend of Asian flavours perfectly complements the duck, and the sugar snap peas add crunch.

SERVES 4

2 boneless duck breasts
15ml/1 tbsp vegetable oil
150g/5oz sugar snap peas
2 carrots, cut into 7.5cm/3in sticks
225g/8oz medium egg noodles
6 spring onions (scallions), sliced
fresh coriander (cilantro) leaves, to garnish

FOR THE MARINADE

15ml/1 tbsp sesame oil
5ml/1 tsp ground coriander
5ml/1 tsp five-spice powder

FOR THE DRESSING

15ml/1 tbsp vinegar
5ml/1 tsp soft light brown sugar
5ml/1 tsp soy sauce
1 garlic clove, crushed
15ml/1 tbsp sesame seeds, toasted
60ml/4 tbsp sunflower oil
ground black pepper

1 Slice the duck breasts thinly widthways and place in a dish. Mix the ingredients for the marinade, pour over the duck and mix. Cover and leave in a cool place for 30 minutes.

2 Heat the oil in a frying pan, add the duck slices and stir-fry for 3–4 minutes, until cooked. Set aside.

3 Bring a pan of water to the boil. Place the sugar snap peas and carrots in a steamer. When the water boils, add the noodles. Place the steamer on top and steam the vegetables. Set the vegetables aside. Drain the noodles, refresh under cold water and drain again. Place in a serving bowl.

4 To make the dressing, mix the vinegar, sugar, soy sauce, garlic and sesame seeds in a bowl. Add pepper, then whisk in the oil. Add to the noodles and mix well. Add the peas, carrots, spring onions and duck slices and toss to mix. Sprinkle the coriander over the top and serve.

Nutritional information per portion: Energy 550kcal/2301kJ; Protein 25.3g; Carbohydrate 47g, of which sugars 4.2g; Fat 31.6g, of which saturates 5.2g; Cholesterol 99mg; Calcium 70mg; Fibre 4.5g; Sodium 192mg.

Warm duck salad with poached eggs

This salad looks spectacular and tastes divine, and makes a perfect celebration first course or, accompanied by warm crusty bread, a light lunch or supper dish.

SERVES 4

3 skinless, boneless duck breasts, thinly
   sliced
30ml/2 tbsp soy sauce
30ml/2 tbsp balsamic vinegar
30ml/2 tbsp groundnut (peanut) oil
25g/1oz/2 tbsp unsalted butter

1 shallot, finely chopped
115g/4oz/1½ cups chanterelle mushrooms
4 eggs
50g/2oz mixed salad leaves
salt and ground black pepper
30ml/2 tbsp extra virgin olive oil, to serve

1 Toss the duck in the soy sauce and balsamic vinegar. Cover and chill for 30 minutes to allow the duck to infuse in the soy sauce and vinegar. Meanwhile, soak 12 bamboo skewers (about 13cm/5in long) in water to help prevent them from burning during cooking.

2 Preheat the grill (broiler). Thread the duck slices on to the skewers, pleating them neatly. Place on a grill pan and drizzle with half the oil. Grill (broil) for 3–5 minutes, then turn the skewers and drizzle with the remaining oil. Grill for a further 3 minutes, or until the duck is cooked through and golden.

3 Meanwhile, melt the butter in a frying pan and cook the finely chopped shallot until softened but not coloured. Add the chanterelle mushrooms and cook over a high heat for about 5 minutes, stirring occasionally.

4 Poach the eggs while the chanterelles are cooking. Half fill a frying pan with water, add salt and heat until simmering. Break the eggs one at a time into a cup before dropping carefully into the water. Poach the eggs gently for about 3 minutes, or until the whites are set. Use a draining spoon to transfer the eggs to a warm plate and trim off any untidy white.

5 Arrange the salad leaves on serving plates, then add the chanterelles and skewered duck. Carefully add the poached eggs. Drizzle with olive oil and season with freshly ground black pepper, then serve at once.

Nutritional information per portion: Energy 271kcal/1132kJ; Protein 29.2g; Carbohydrate 1.5g, of which sugars 1.1g; Fat 18.6g, of which saturates 3.9g; Cholesterol 314mg; Calcium 51mg; Fibre 0.7g; Sodium 196mg.

Meat Salads

The beauty of these meat salads is that they are main dishes; many include rice, potatoes or pasta so they are perfect for a hearty meal. For a delicious summery lunch, try Asparagus and Bacon Salad, or for a more substantial repast, Crunchy Salad with Black Pudding would be ideal. Waldorf Rice Salad is satisfying and tasty with a mixture of aromatic herbs and crunchy nuts.

Warm salad of bayonne ham and new potatoes

With a lightly spiced nutty dressing, this warm salad is as delicious as it is fashionable, and an excellent choice for informal entertaining.

SERVES 4

225g/8oz new potatoes, halved if large
50g/2oz green beans
115g/4oz young spinach leaves
2 spring onions (scallions), sliced
4 eggs, hard-boiled and quartered
50g/2oz Bayonne ham, cut into strips
juice of ½ lemon
salt and ground black pepper

FOR THE DRESSING

60ml/4 tbsp olive oil
5ml/1 tsp ground turmeric
5ml/1 tsp ground cumin
50g/2oz/⅓ cup shelled hazelnuts

1 Cook the potatoes in boiling salted water for 10–15 minutes, or until tender, then drain well. Cook the beans in boiling salted water for 2 minutes, until just tender, then drain.

2 Toss the potatoes and beans with the spinach and spring onions in a bowl.

3 Arrange the hard-boiled egg quarters on the salad and lay the strips of ham over the top. Sprinkle with the lemon juice and season with plenty of salt and pepper.

4 Heat the dressing ingredients in a large frying pan and cook, stirring frequently, until the nuts turn golden. Pour the hot, nutty dressing over the salad and serve at once.

Nutritional information per portion: Energy 323kcal/1341kJ; Protein 12.4g; Carbohydrate 10.9g, of which sugars 2.2g; Fat 25.8g, of which saturates 4.2g; Cholesterol 199mg; Calcium 105mg; Fibre 2.3g; Sodium 270mg.

Omelette and bacon salad

Rich duck eggs produce an omelette with a lovely, delicate flavour, which combines perfectly with crispy bacon and fresh leaves in this elegant salad.

SERVES 4

6 streaky (fatty) bacon rashers (strips),
    rinds removed and chopped
2 duck eggs
2 spring onions (scallions), chopped
few sprigs of fresh coriander
    (cilantro), chopped
25g/1oz/2 tbsp butter
400g/14oz mixed salad leaves
60ml/4 tbsp olive oil
30ml/2 tbsp balsamic vinegar
salt and ground black pepper

1 Warm an omelette pan over a low heat and gently fry the chopped bacon until the fat runs. Increase the heat to crisp up the bacon, stirring frequently. When the bacon pieces are brown and crispy, remove from the heat and transfer to a hot dish to keep warm.

2 Beat the eggs with the spring onions and coriander and season with salt and pepper.

3 Melt the butter in the cleaned omelette pan and pour in the egg mixture. Cook for 2–3 minutes to make an unfolded omelette. Remove the omelette from the pan and set the pan aside. Carefully cut the omelette into long strips.

4 Place the salad leaves in a large salad bowl. Add the omelette strips to the salad with the bacon. Pour the oil and vinegar into the omelette pan, with salt and pepper, stir together, then heat briefly and pour over the salad. Toss well before serving.

Nutritional information per portion: Energy 301kcal/1246kJ; Protein 12.4g; Carbohydrate 1.8g, of which sugars 1.8g; Fat 27.3g, of which saturates 8.4g; Cholesterol 288mg; Calcium 55mg; Fibre 0.9g; Sodium 664mg.

Asparagus and bacon salad

Serve this stylish salad as a light lunch or supper or simply to add interest to plainly roasted or steamed chicken or fish.

SERVES 4

500g/1¼lb medium asparagus spears
130g/4½oz thin-cut smoked back
   (lean) bacon
250g/9oz chicory (Belgian endive) leaves
   or other bitter-tasting leaves

FOR THE FRENCH DRESSING

30ml/2 tbsp white wine vinegar
90ml/6 tbsp extra virgin olive oil
5ml/1 tsp Dijon mustard
pinch of sugar
salt and ground black pepper

1 Trim off any tough stalk ends from the asparagus and cut the spears into three. Set apart the tender tips.

2 Heat a 1cm/½in depth of water in a frying pan until simmering. Reserve the asparagus tips and cook the remainder of the spears for about 3 minutes, until almost tender. Add the tips and cook for 1 minute more. Drain and refresh under cold running water.

3 To make the dressing, whisk the vinegar, oil, mustard and sugar. Season with salt and pepper.

4 Dry-fry the bacon until golden and crisp and then set it aside to cool slightly. Use kitchen scissors to snip it into bitesize pieces. Place the salad leaves in a bowl and add the bacon.

5 Add the asparagus spears and the asparagus tips and a little black pepper to the salad leaves and bacon. Pour the dressing over and toss the salad lightly. Serve at once.

Nutritional information per portion: Energy 259kcal/1068kJ; Protein 9.5g; Carbohydrate 3.6g, of which sugars 3.5g; Fat 23g, of which saturates 4.6g; Cholesterol 17mg; Calcium 53mg; Fibre 2.7g; Sodium 519mg.

Warm potato salad with bacon dressing

This tasty summer salad becomes a favourite with all who try it. Use real new-season potatoes rather than all-year 'baby' potatoes, if possible, and also dry-cured bacon.

SERVES 4–6

900g/2lb small new potatoes

sprig of mint

15–30ml/1–2 tbsp olive oil

1 onion, chopped

175g/6oz streaky (fatty) or back (lean) bacon, diced

2 garlic cloves, crushed

30ml/2 tbsp chopped fresh parsley

a small bunch of chives, chopped

15ml/1 tbsp wine vinegar or cider vinegar

15ml/1 tbsp Irish wholegrain mustard

salt and ground black pepper

1 Scrape or rub off the skins from the new potatoes, and cook in salted water with the mint for about 10 minutes, or until just tender. Drain and allow to cool a little, then turn into a salad bowl.

2 Heat the oil in a frying pan, then add the onion and cook gently until just softening. Add the diced bacon to the pan and cook for 3–5 minutes, until beginning to crisp up.

3 Add the garlic and cook for another minute or so, and then add the chopped herbs, the vinegar, mustard and seasoning to taste, remembering that the bacon may be salty.

4 Pour the dressing over the potatoes. Toss gently to mix, and serve warm.

Nutritional information per portion: Energy 264kcal/1112kJ; Protein 13.3g; Carbohydrate 39.9g, of which sugars 5.6g; Fat 6.8g, of which saturates 1.7g; Cholesterol 14mg; Calcium 76mg; Fibre 4g; Sodium 625mg.

Peruvian salad

With its vibrantly coloured ingredients, this really is a spectacular-looking salad. It could be served as a side dish or would make a delicious light lunch. In Peru, white rice would be used, but brown rice adds an interesting texture and flavour.

SERVES 4

115g/4oz/1 cup long grain brown or white
   rice, cooked
15ml/1 tbsp chopped fresh parsley
1 red (bell) pepper
1 small onion, sliced
olive oil, for sprinkling
115g/4oz green beans, halved
50g/2oz/½ cup baby corn
4 quail's eggs, hard-boiled
25–50g/1–2oz Spanish ham, cut into
   thin slices
1 small avocado
lemon juice, for sprinkling

75g/3oz mixed salad leaves
15ml/1 tbsp capers
about 10 stuffed olives, halved

FOR THE DRESSING

1 garlic clove, crushed
60ml/4 tbsp olive oil
45ml/3 tbsp sunflower oil
30ml/2 tbsp lemon juice
45ml/3 tbsp natural (plain) yogurt
2.5ml/½ tsp mustard
2.5ml/½ tsp sugar
salt and freshly ground black pepper

1 Make the dressing: put all the ingredients in a bowl and whisk with a fork until smooth. Alternatively, shake the ingredients together in a screw-top jar.

2 Put the cooked rice into a large salad bowl and spoon in half the dressing. Add the chopped parsley, stir well and set aside.

3 Cut the pepper in half, remove the seeds and pith, then place the halves, cut side down, in a small roasting pan. Add the onion rings. Sprinkle the onion with a little olive oil, place the pan under a hot grill (broiler) and grill (broil) for 5–6 minutes until the pepper blackens and blisters and the onion turns golden. You may need to stir the onion once or twice so that it grills evenly.

4 Stir the onion in with the rice. Put the pepper in a plastic bag and knot the bag. When the steam has loosened the skin on the pepper halves and they are cool enough to handle, peel them and cut the flesh into thin strips.

5 Cook the green beans in boiling water for 2 minutes, then add the corn and cook for 1–2 minutes more, until tender. Drain both vegetables, refresh them under cold water, then drain again. Place in a large mixing bowl and add the red pepper strips, quail's eggs and ham.

6 Peel the avocado, remove the stone (pit), and cut the flesh into slices or chunks. Sprinkle with the lemon juice. Put the salad leaves in a separate mixing bowl, add the avocado and mix lightly. Arrange the salad on top of the rice.

7 Stir about 45ml/3 tbsp of the remaining dressing into the green bean and pepper mixture. Pile this on top of the salad.

8 Sprinkle the capers and stuffed olives on top and serve the salad with the remaining dressing.

Nutritional information per portion: Energy 415kcal/1726kJ; Protein 9.1g; Carbohydrate 52.8g, of which sugars 6.6g; Fat 18.5g, of which saturates 3.2g; Cholesterol 48mg; Calcium 77mg; Fibre 3.3g; Sodium 417mg.

Crunchy salad with black pudding

Fried until crisp, slices of black pudding add an interesting dimension to salads, particularly with crunchy croûtons and sweet cherry tomatoes.

SERVES 4

250g/9oz black pudding (blood
    sausage), sliced
1 focaccia loaf, plain or flavoured with
    sun-dried tomatoes, garlic and herbs
45ml/3 tbsp olive oil
1 cos or romaine lettuce, torn into
    bitesize pieces
250g/9oz cherry tomatoes, halved

FOR THE DRESSING

juice of 1 lemon
90ml/6 tbsp olive oil
10ml/2 tsp French mustard
15ml/1 tbsp clear honey
30ml/2 tbsp chopped fresh herbs
salt and ground black pepper

1 Dry-fry the black pudding in a large, non-stick frying pan for 5–10 minutes, or until browned and crisp, turning occasionally. Remove the black pudding from the pan using a slotted spoon and drain on sheets of kitchen paper. Set aside.

2 Cut the focaccia into chunks. Add the oil to the juices in the frying pan and cook the focaccia in two batches, turning often, until golden on all sides. Drain the focaccia on kitchen paper.

3 Mix together the focaccia, black pudding, lettuce and cherry tomatoes in a large serving bowl.

4 Whisk together the dressing ingredients, seasoning with salt and pepper. Toss the dressing into the salad and serve.

Nutritional information per portion: Energy 702kcal/2936kJ; Protein 17.2g; Carbohydrate 67.4g, of which sugars 8.3g; Fat 42.3g, of which saturates 9.5g; Cholesterol 43mg; Calcium 204mg; Fibre 3.2g; Sodium 1132mg.

Warm salad with ham, egg and asparagus

When you think it's too hot for pasta, try serving it in a warm salad. Here it is combined with ham, eggs and asparagus, with a tangy mustard dressing that includes the asparagus stems.

SERVES 4

450g/1lb asparagus
450g/1lb dried tagliatelle
225g/8oz cooked ham, in 5mm/¼in thick slices, cut into fingers
2 hard-boiled eggs, sliced
50g/2oz fresh Parmesan cheese, shaved
salt and ground black pepper

FOR THE DRESSING

50g/2oz cooked potato
75ml/5 tbsp extra virgin olive oil
15ml/1 tbsp lemon juice
10ml/2 tsp Dijon mustard
120ml/4fl oz/½ cup vegetable stock

1 Trim and discard the tough woody part of the asparagus. Cut the spears in half and cook the thicker stems in boiling salted water for 12 minutes. After 6 minutes add the tips. Drain, then refresh the asparagus under cold water until warm.

2 Finely chop 150g/5oz of the thick asparagus pieces. Place in a food processor with all the dressing ingredients and process until smooth.

3 Cook the pasta in a large pan of lightly salted boiling water according to the packet instructions, until al dente. Refresh under cold running water until just luke warm, then drain.

4 Toss the pasta with the asparagus sauce and divide between four plates. Top with the ham, hard-boiled eggs and asparagus tips. Serve with a sprinkling of Parmesan cheese shavings.

Nutritional information per portion: Energy 696kcal/2928kJ; Protein 35g; Carbohydrate 88g, of which sugars 6.3g; Fat 25.1g, of which saturates 6.3g; Cholesterol 140mg; Calcium 224mg; Fibre 5.1g; Sodium 852mg.

Waldorf rice salad

Waldorf Salad takes its name from the Waldorf Hotel in New York, where it was invented. The rice makes this salad substantial enough to serve as a main course for two people.

SERVES 2–4

115g/4oz/generous ¹/₂ cup white long
    grain rice
1 red apple
1 green apple
60ml/4 tbsp lemon juice
3 celery sticks
2–3 slices thick cooked ham
90ml/6 tbsp good quality mayonnaise,
    preferably home-made
60ml/4 tbsp sour cream
generous pinch of saffron, dissolved in
    15ml/1 tbsp hot water
10ml/2 tsp chopped fresh basil
15ml/1 tbsp chopped fresh parsley
several romaine or iceberg lettuce leaves
50g/2oz/¹/₂ cup walnuts, roughly
    chopped
salt and ground black pepper

1 Cook the rice in boiling water until tender. Drain and set aside to cool.

2 Cut the apples into quarters, core and finely slice one red and one green apple quarter. Place the slices in a bowl with half the lemon juice and reserve for the garnish. Peel the remaining apple quarters and cut into fine sticks. Place in a separate bowl and toss with another 15ml/1 tbsp of lemon juice.

3 Cut the celery into thin strips. Roll up each slice of ham, slice finely and add to the apple sticks, with the celery.

4 Mix together the mayonnaise, sour cream and saffron water. Stir in salt and pepper to taste. Stir into the rice with the herbs. Add the apple and celery and the remaining lemon juice.

5 Arrange the lettuce leaves in a salad bowl and pile the rice and apple mixture into it. Sprinkle with the walnuts and garnish with apple slices.

Nutritional information per portion: Energy 523kcal/2178kJ; Protein 24.7g; Carbohydrate 32.4g, of which sugars 9.3g; Fat 32.9g, of which saturates 6.4g; Cholesterol 84mg; Calcium 111mg; Fibre 3.2g; Sodium 1331mg.

Mushroom, bean and chorizo salad

This mixture of spicy sausage, tender, sweet beans and delicate mushrooms is delicious. Serve with plain fish or chicken dishes, or offer with crusty bread as a hearty lunch or supper dish.

SERVES 4

225g/8oz shelled broad (fava) beans
175g/6oz frying chorizo
60ml/4 tbsp extra virgin olive oil
225g/8oz/3 cups brown cap (cremini)
  mushrooms, sliced
60ml/4 tbsp chopped fresh chives
salt and ground black pepper

1 Cook the broad beans in a pan of salted boiling water for 7–8 minutes. Drain and refresh under cold water.

2 Remove the skin from the sausage. If it doesn't peel off easily, score along the length of the sausage with a sharp knife first. Cut the chorizo into small chunks. Heat the oil in a small pan, add the chorizo and cook for 2–3 minutes.

3 Put the sliced mushrooms in a bowl and add the chorizo and oil. Toss to combine, then leave to cool.

4 If the beans are large, peel away the tough outer skins. Stir the beans and half the chives into the mushroom mixture, and season with salt and pepper to taste. Serve at room temperature, garnished with the remaining chives.

Nutritional information per portion: Energy 283kcal/1174kJ; Protein 9.7g; Carbohydrate 11.9g, of which sugars 1.6g; Fat 22.2g, of which saturates 6.1g; Cholesterol 18mg; Calcium 56mg; Fibre 4.5g; Sodium 362mg.

Warm chorizo and spinach salad

Spanish chorizo sausage contributes an intense spiciness to this hearty warm salad. Spinach leaves have enough flavour to compete with the chorizo and add extra colour.

SERVES 4

225g/8oz baby spinach leaves
90ml/6 tbsp extra virgin olive oil
150g/5oz chorizo sausage, very
    thinly sliced
30ml/2 tbsp sherry vinegar
salt and ground black pepper

1 Discard any tough stalks from the spinach. Pour the oil into a large frying pan and add the chorizo sausage. Cook gently for 3 minutes, until the sausage slices start to shrivel slightly and begin to colour.

2 Add the spinach leaves and remove the pan from the heat. Toss the spinach in the warm oil until it just starts to wilt.

3 Add the sherry vinegar and a little salt and pepper. Toss the ingredients briefly, then serve immediately, while still warm.

Nutritional information per portion: Energy 300kcal/1238kJ; Protein 5.6g; Carbohydrate 4.5g, of which sugars 1.4g; Fat 29g, of which saturates 7g; Cholesterol 18mg; Calcium 111mg; Fibre 1.4g; Sodium 364mg.

Pasta salad with salami

This salad is simple to make and it can be prepared in advance and kept in the refrigerator for a few hours, adding the dressing just before serving.

SERVES 4

225g/8oz dried fusilli

275g/10oz jar charcoal-roasted peppers
    in oil

115g/4oz/1 cup pitted black olives

4 sun-dried tomatoes, quartered

115g/4oz Roquefort cheese, crumbled

10 slices peppered salami, cut into strips

115g/4oz mixed salad leaves

30ml/2 tbsp white wine vinegar

30ml/2 tbsp chopped fresh oregano

2 garlic cloves, crushed

salt and ground black pepper

1 Cook the pasta in a large pan of lightly salted boiling water according to the instructions on the packet, until al dente. Drain thoroughly and rinse with cold water, then drain again.

2 Drain the peppers and reserve 60ml/4 tbsp of the oil for the dressing. Cut the peppers into long, fine strips and mix them with the olives, sun-dried tomatoes and Roquefort in a large bowl. Stir in the pasta and peppered salami.

3 Divide the salad leaves between four individual bowls and spoon the pasta salad on top. Whisk the reserved oil with the wine vinegar, oregano and garlic. Season with salt and pepper to taste, then spoon over the salad and serve immediately.

Nutritional information per portion: Energy 429kcal/1797kJ; Protein 17.8g; Carbohydrate 46.7g, of which sugars 6.6g; Fat 20.3g, of which saturates 8.9g; Cholesterol 37mg; Calcium 188mg; Fibre 3.9g; Sodium 1341mg.

Saeng wa of grilled pork

Pork fillet is cut in strips, before being grilled, in this tasty Thai dish. Shredded and then tossed with a delicious sweet-sour sauce, it makes a marvellous warm salad.

SERVES 4

30ml/2 tbsp dark soy sauce
15ml/1 tbsp clear honey
400g/14oz pork fillet (tenderloin)
6 shallots, very thinly sliced lengthways
1 lemon grass stalk, thinly sliced
5 kaffir lime leaves, thinly sliced
5cm/2in piece fresh root ginger, peeled
  and sliced into fine shreds
1/2 fresh long red chilli, seeded and sliced
  into fine shreds
a small bunch of fresh coriander
  (cilantro), chopped

FOR THE DRESSING

30ml/2 tbsp palm sugar (jaggery) or
  light muscovado (brown) sugar
30ml/2 tbsp Thai fish sauce
juice of 2 limes
20ml/4 tsp thick tamarind juice, made by
  mixing tamarind paste with warm water

1 Preheat the grill (broiler) to medium. Mix the soy sauce with the honey in a small bowl or jug (pitcher) and stir until completely blended.

2 Cut the pork fillet lengthways into quarters to make four long, thick strips. Place in a grill pan. Brush generously with the soy sauce and honey mixture, then grill (broil) for 10–15 minutes, until cooked through and tender. Turn the strips over frequently and baste with the soy sauce and honey mixture.

3 Transfer the cooked pork strips to a chopping board. Slice the meat across the grain, then shred it with a fork. Place in a large bowl and add the shallot slices, lemon grass, kaffir lime leaves, ginger, chilli and chopped coriander.

4 Make the dressing. Place the sugar, fish sauce, lime juice and tamarind juice in a bowl. Whisk together until the sugar has completely dissolved. Pour the dressing over the pork mixture and toss well to mix, then serve.

Nutritional information per portion: Energy 170kcal/718kJ; Protein 22g; Carbohydrate 12.2g, of which sugars 12.1g; Fat 4g, of which saturates 1.4g; Cholesterol 63mg; Calcium 16mg; Fibre 0.2g; Sodium 873mg.

Beef and mushroom salad

All of the ingredients you will need to make this traditional Thai dish – known as yam nua yang *– are widely available in larger supermarkets.*

SERVES 4

675g/1¹/₂lb fillet (tenderloin) or
   rump (round) steak
30ml/2 tbsp olive oil
2 small mild red chillies, seeded
   and sliced
225g/8oz/3¹/₄ cups shiitake mushrooms,
   stems removed and caps sliced

FOR THE DRESSING

3 spring onions (scallions),
   finely chopped
2 garlic cloves, finely chopped
juice of 1 lime
15–30ml/1–2 tbsp Thai fish sauce
5ml/1 tsp soft light brown sugar
30ml/2 tbsp chopped fresh
   coriander (cilantro)

TO SERVE

1 cos or romaine lettuce, torn
   into strips
175g/6oz cherry tomatoes, halved
5cm/2in piece cucumber, peeled,
   halved and thinly sliced
45ml/3 tbsp toasted
   sesame seeds

1 Preheat the grill (broiler) to medium, then cook the steak for 2–4 minutes on each side. (In Thailand, beef is traditionally served quite rare.) Leave the steak to cool for at least 15 minutes.

2 Slice the meat as thinly as possible and place the slices in a bowl.

3 Heat the olive oil in a frying pan. Add the seeded and sliced red chillies and the sliced shiitake mushroom caps. Cook for 5 minutes, stirring occasionally.

4 Turn off the heat and add the steak slices to the pan. Stir well to coat the steak slices in the chilli and mushroom mixture.

5 Make the dressing by mixing all the ingredients together in a bowl, then pour it over the meat mixture and toss gently.

6 Arrange the lettuce, tomatoes and cucumber on a serving plate. Spoon the steak mixture on to the centre of the salad and sprinkle the sesame seeds over the top. Serve at once.

Nutritional information per portion: Energy 381kcal/1588kJ; Protein 39.7g; Carbohydrate 4g, of which sugars 3.8g; Fat 23g, of which saturates 6.6g; Cholesterol 103mg; Calcium 105mg; Fibre 2.4g; Sodium 352mg.

Thai beef salad

This luxurious salad combines tender strips of sirloin steak with a wonderfully piquant Thai chilli and lime dressing. It can be served at room temperature or chilled.

SERVES 4

2 sirloin steaks, each about 225g/8oz

1 lemon grass stalk, root trimmed

1 red onion or 4 Thai shallots, thinly sliced

1/2 cucumber, cut into strips

30ml/2 tbsp chopped spring onion (scallion)

juice of 2 limes

15–30ml/1–2 tbsp Thai fish sauce

2–4 fresh red chillies, seeded and finely chopped

Chinese mustard cress, salad cress or fresh coriander (cilantro), to garnish

1 Dry-fry the steaks in a large frying pan over a medium heat. Cook for 4–6 minutes for rare, 6–8 minutes for medium-rare and 10 minutes for well done, depending on their thickness. Alternatively, cook under a preheated grill (broiler). Remove the steaks from the pan and leave to rest for 10–15 minutes. Meanwhile, cut off the lower 5cm/2in from the lemon grass stalk and chop finely.

2 When the meat is cool, slice thinly and put in a large bowl. Add the sliced onion or shallots, cucumber, lemon grass and chopped spring onion to the meat slices.

3 Toss the salad and add lime juice and fish sauce to taste. Add the red chillies and mix. Transfer to a serving bowl or plate. Serve, garnished with the Chinese mustard cress, salad cress or coriander leaves.

Nutritional information per portion: Energy 161kcal/674kJ; Protein 26.9g; Carbohydrate 1.8g, of which sugars 1.4g; Fat 5.1g, of which saturates 2.3g; Cholesterol 57mg; Calcium 14mg; Fibre 0.3g; Sodium 347mg.

Seared beef salad in a lime dressing

Versions of this dish are enjoyed all over South-east Asia. In this favourite dish, strips of seared beef are flavoured with lime and chilli, then tossed with crunchy beansprouts and fresh herbs.

Serves 4

about 7.5ml/1¹⁄₂ tsp vegetable oil

450g/1lb beef fillet, cut into steaks
    2.5cm/1in thick

115g/4oz/¹⁄₂ cup beansprouts

a bunch each of fresh basil and mint,
    stalks removed, leaves shredded

1 lime, cut into slices, to serve

FOR THE DRESSING

grated rind and juice (about 80ml/3fl oz)
    of 2 limes

30ml/2 tbsp Thai fish sauce

30ml/2 tbsp demerara (raw) sugar

2 garlic cloves, crushed

2 lemon grass stalks, finely sliced

2 fresh red Serrano chillies, seeded and
    finely sliced

1 To make the dressing, beat the lime rind, juice and fish sauce in a bowl with the sugar, until the sugar dissolves. Stir in the garlic, lemon grass and chillies and set aside.

2 Pour a little oil into a heavy pan and rub it over the base with a piece of kitchen paper. Heat the pan and sear the steaks for 1–2 minutes each side.

3 Transfer the steaks to a board and leave to cool a little. Using a sharp knife, cut the meat into thin slices. Toss the slices in the dressing, cover and leave to marinate for 1–2 hours.

4 Drain the meat of any excess juice and transfer it to a wide serving bowl. Add the beansprouts and herbs and toss it all together. Serve with lime slices to squeeze over.

Nutritional information per portion: Energy 233kcal/979kJ; Protein 26g; carbohydate 12g, of which sugars 9g; Fat 9g, of which saturates 3g; Cholesterol 69mg; Calcium 74mg; Fibre 0.5g; Sodium 400mg.

Thai-style rare beef and mango salad

This simplified version of Thai beef salad is especially tasty when accompanied by little bowls of ingredients at the table to sprinkle over the salad. Your guests will appreciate the addition of fresh coriander (cilantro) leaves, chopped spring onions (scallions) and peanuts.

SERVES 4

450g/1lb sirloin steak
45ml/3 tbsp garlic-infused olive oil
45ml/3 tbsp soy sauce

2 mangoes, peeled, stoned (pitted) and
    finely sliced
ground black pepper

1 Put the steak in a shallow, non-metallic dish and pour over the oil and soy sauce. Season with pepper and turn the steaks to coat in the marinade. Cover and chill for 2 hours.

2 Heat a griddle pan until hot. Remove the steak from the marinade and place on the griddle pan. Cook for 3–5 minutes on each side, moving the steak halfway through if you want a criss-cross pattern.

3 Transfer the steak to a board and leave to rest for 5–10 minutes. Meanwhile, pour the marinade into the pan and cook for a few seconds, then remove from the heat.

4 Thinly slice the steak and arrange on four serving plates with the mangoes. Drizzle over the pan juices and serve immediately.

Nutritional information per portion: Energy 286kcal/1200kJ; Protein 27.4g; Carbohydrate 14.7g, of which sugars 14.4g; Fat 13.5g, of which saturates 3.5g; Cholesterol 57mg; Calcium 19mg; Fibre 2.6g; Sodium 615mg.

COOK'S TIP
• *When shopping for this recipe, choose good quality beef from a reputable butcher or supplier.*

Beef and sweet potato salad

This salad is an unusual and delicious way to serve beef fillet. The piquant, fresh-tasting dressing is a good foil for the peppery beef. This recipe makes a good main dish for a summer buffet.

SERVES 6–8

800g/1¾lb fillet of beef
5ml/1 tsp black peppercorns, crushed
10ml/2 tsp chopped fresh thyme
60ml/4 tbsp olive oil
450g/1lb orange-fleshed sweet potato,
    peeled and sliced
salt and ground black pepper

FOR THE DRESSING

1 garlic clove, chopped
15g/½oz flat leaf parsley
30ml/2 tbsp chopped fresh
    coriander (cilantro)
15ml/1 tbsp small salted capers, rinsed
½–1 fresh green chilli, seeded
    and chopped
10ml/2 tsp Dijon mustard
10–15ml/2–3 tsp white wine vinegar
75ml/5 tbsp extra virgin olive oil
2 shallots, finely chopped

1 Roll the beef fillet in the crushed peppercorns and thyme, then set aside to marinate for a few hours. Preheat the oven to 200°C/400°F/Gas 6.

2 Heat half the olive oil in a frying pan. Add the beef and brown it all over, turning often, to seal. Place on a baking tray and cook in the oven for 15 minutes. Remove from the oven, cover with foil, and rest for 15 minutes.

3 Meanwhile, preheat the grill (broiler). Brush the sweet potato with the remaining olive oil, season with salt and pepper, and grill (broil) for about 5–6 minutes on each side, until browned. Cut into strips and place them in a bowl. Cut the beef into slices or strips and toss with the sweet potato.

4 To make the dressing, process the garlic, parsley, coriander, capers, chilli, mustard and 10ml/2 tsp of the vinegar in a food processor. With the motor still running, pour in the oil to make a smooth dressing. Season and add more vinegar, to taste. Stir in the shallots.

5 Add the dressing to the sweet potatoes and beef. Serve after 2 hours.

Nutritional information per portion: Energy 300kcal/1253kJ; Protein 21.9g; Carbohydrate 12g, of which sugars 3.2g; Fat 18.6g, of which saturates 4.6g; Cholesterol 61mg; Calcium 18mg; Fibre 1.4g; Sodium 67mg.

Bamboo shoot salad with persimmon dressing

Persimmon, if you use a ripe one, adds a tangy sweetness to both the seasoning and the dressing for this beautiful salad.

SERVES 1–2

2 dried shiitake mushrooms
50g/2oz beef flank, thinly sliced
25ml/1½ tbsp vegetable oil
90g/3½oz/½ cup beansprouts
200g/7oz bamboo shoots
1 egg, beaten
90g/3½oz watercress or rocket (arugula)
salt
½ red chilli, seeded and sliced, to garnish

FOR THE SEASONING

7.5ml/1½ tsp dark soy sauce
10g/¼oz red persimmon, finely chopped
½ spring onion (scallion), finely chopped
1 garlic clove, crushed
5ml/1 tsp sesame seeds
2.5ml/½ tsp sesame oil

FOR THE DRESSING

60ml/4 tbsp dark soy sauce
30ml/2 tbsp rice vinegar
40g/1½oz red persimmon, chopped
5ml/1 tsp sesame seeds

1 Soak the mushrooms in warm water for 30 minutes, until softened. When they are soft, drain and thinly slice them, discarding the stems. Put them, with the beef slices, in a bowl. Add the seasoning ingredients and mix well.

2 Stir-fry the beef and mushrooms in 15ml/1 tbsp of oil over a medium heat until cooked, then remove, cool and chill.

3 Trim the beansprouts and blanch in boiling water for 3 minutes. Drain. Do the same to the chopped bamboo shoots.

4 Combine all the dressing ingredients in a bowl and set aside.

5 Coat a frying pan with oil, season the egg and make a thin omelette. Remove from the pan and cut into thin strips.

6 Arrange the beef on a plate with the bamboo shoots, watercress or rocket and beansprouts. Garnish with the sliced chilli and egg strips before serving with the dressing.

Nutritional information per portion: Energy 268kcal/1115kJ; Protein 17g; Carbohydrate 9.1g, of which sugars 6.1g; Fat 18.6g, of which saturates3.6g; Cholesterol 119mg; Calcium 164mg; Fibre 3.5g; Sodium 2489mg.

Cambodian raw beef salad with peanuts

This Cambodian beef salad has a distinctive taste as it uses the flavourful fish extract, tuk prahoc. Serve with rice noodles and stir-fried vegetables for an impressive dinner party dish.

SERVES 4

45ml/3 tbsp tuk prahoc
juice of 3 limes
45ml/3 tbsp sugar
2 lemon grass stalks, trimmed and
    finely sliced
2 shallots, peeled and finely sliced
2 garlic cloves, finely chopped
450g/1lb beef fillet, very finely sliced
1 fresh red chilli, seeded and finely sliced
50g/2oz roasted, unsalted peanuts, finely
    chopped or crushed
a small bunch of fresh coriander
    (cilantro), finely chopped, plus extra
    leaves, to garnish

1 In a bowl, beat 30ml/2 tbsp tuk prahoc with the juice of 2 limes and 30ml/2 tbsp of the sugar, until the sugar has dissolved. Add the lemon grass, shallots and garlic and mix well.

2 Toss the lime mixture with the slices of beef, then cover and place in the refrigerator for 1–2 hours.

3 Meanwhile, in a small bowl, beat the remaining tuk prahoc with the juice of the third lime. Stir in the remaining sugar and set aside.

4 Put the beef slices, drained of any remaining liquid, in a clean bowl. Add the chilli, peanuts and coriander. Toss with the dressing, garnish with coriander and serve.

Nutritional information per portion: Energy 321kcal/1343kJ; Protein 29g; Carbohydrate 15g, of which sugars 14g; Fat 16g, of which saturates 5g; Cholesterol 65mg; Calcium 48mg; Fibre 1.6g; Sodium 78mg.

Marinated beef and potato salad

The beef steak needs to marinate overnight, but once that has been done, this dish is very quick to assemble and makes a substantial main course.

SERVES 6

900g/2lb sirloin steak
3 large white potatoes
1/2 red (bell) pepper, seeded and diced
1/2 green (bell) pepper, seeded and diced
1 small red onion, finely chopped
2 garlic cloves, crushed
4 spring onions (scallions),
   diagonally sliced
1 small cos or romaine lettuce,
   leaves torn
salt and ground black pepper
olive oil, to serve
Parmesan cheese shavings, to serve

FOR THE MARINADE
120ml/4fl oz/1/2 cup olive oil
120ml/4fl oz/1/2 cup red wine vinegar
90ml/6 tbsp soy sauce

1 Place the beef in a large, non-metallic container. Mix together the marinade ingredients. Season with pepper and pour over the meat.

2 Cover the meat and leave to marinate for several hours, or preferably overnight.

3 Drain the marinade from the meat and pat the joint dry. Preheat a frying pan, cut the meat carefully into thin slices and fry for a few minutes until just cooked on each side, but still slightly pink. Set aside to cool.

4 Using a melon baller, scoop out rounds from each potato. Boil in lightly salted water for 5 minutes or until just tender.

5 Drain the potatoes and transfer to a bowl. Add the peppers, onion, garlic, spring onions and lettuce leaves. Season with salt and pepper and toss together.

6 Transfer the potato and pepper mixture to a plate with the beef. Drizzle with a little extra olive oil and serve topped with the Parmesan shavings.

Nutritional information per portion: Energy 296kcal/1247kJ; Protein 38g; Carbohydrate 20.1g, of which sugars 5g; Fat 7.6g, of which saturates 3.2g; Cholesterol 77mg; Calcium 40mg; Fibre 2.3g; Sodium 120mg.

Rabbit salad with ruby chard

Chard is a delicious vegetable and can be used instead of spinach in many recipes. The leaf has a great colour, especially in the ruby varieties, which is a deep red. Prepare it as you would spinach.

SERVES 4

15ml/1 tbsp groundnut (peanut) oil
2 saddles of rabbit, each weighing
    approximately 250g/9oz
250g/9oz mixed salad leaves
50g/2oz/¼ cup butter
225g/8oz ruby chard leaves,
    stalks removed
salt and ground black pepper

FOR THE DRESSING

5ml/1 tsp balsamic vinegar
45ml/3 tbsp extra virgin olive oil
5ml/1 tsp Dijon mustard
salt and ground black pepper

1 Heat a frying pan and pour in the oil, allowing it to get quite hot. Dry and season the saddles of rabbit and place them skin side down. Reduce the heat and brown lightly in the pan.

2 Turn the saddles over on to the rib side, cover and cook over a very low heat for about 7 minutes. Remove from the heat, and leave to rest.

3 Place the salad leaves in a bowl. Mix the ingredients for the dressing and toss with the leaves. Divide the salad among four individual plates.

4 Remove the rabbit from the pan and return the pan to the hob, melt the butter and add the chard all at once. Season with salt and ground black pepper and toss to coat well with the butter. Once it has wilted – about 3 minutes – it is ready.

5 Slice the rabbit fillets from the back of the saddle and take the small fillets from underneath. Cut thinly and add to the salad. Add the chard and serve.

Nutritional information per portion: Energy 287kcal/1192kJ; Protein 29g; Carbohydrate 1g, of which sugars 0.9g; Fat 18.5g, of which saturates 9.1g; Cholesterol 115mg; Calcium 126mg; Fibre 1.2g; Sodium 238mg.

Hussar's salad

This is a traditional Dutch New Year's Eve dish, so-called because the salad was made up of leftover cold meat and served to visiting soldiers (hussars) calling on female servants.

SERVES 6

1 lettuce, coarse outer leaves removed
600g/1lb 6oz boiled potatoes
about 45ml/3 tbsp vegetable oil
about 45ml/3 tbsp white wine vinegar
5ml/1 tsp Dijon mustard
1 tart apple
4 gherkins, chopped
60ml/4 tbsp cocktail onions, chopped
1 cooked beetroot (beet), peeled
   and diced
300g/11oz cold cooked veal or beef, diced
2 hard-boiled eggs, finely chopped
150–250ml/5–8fl oz/
   ²/₃–1 cup mayonnaise
salt and ground black pepper
15ml/1 tbsp chopped fresh parsley,
   to garnish

1 Wash the lettuce leaves, line a shallow dish with them and set aside.

2 Mash the potatoes with the oil, vinegar and mustard in a bowl until smooth and season with salt and pepper. Add more oil and vinegar, if needed.

3 Peel and dice the apple. Set aside 15ml/1 tbsp each of the gherkins, onions and beetroot for the garnish.

4 Carefully mix the remainder with the mashed potato, then stir in the apple, meat and eggs.

5 Make a mountain of this mixture over the lettuce leaves, and then cover with a thick coating of mayonnaise.

6 Garnish with the reserved beetroot, gherkins and onions and sprinkle with the parsley before serving.

Nutritional information per portion: Energy 425kcal/1768kJ; Protein 16.3g; Carbohydrate 20.5g, of which sugars 5.2g; Fat 31.5g, of which saturates 6.1g; Cholesterol 111mg; Calcium 39mg; Fibre 2g; Sodium 217mg.

Strawberry and smoked venison salad

The combination of strawberries, balsamic vinegar and smoked venison creates a perfect ménage à trois. The tang of the vinegar sets off the sweetness of the strawberries, which must be ripe, and adds a fruity contrast to the rich, dry, smoky venison.

SERVES 4

12 large strawberries
2.5ml/¹/₂ tsp caster (superfine) sugar
5ml/1 tsp balsamic vinegar
8 thin slices of smoked venison
225g/8oz mixed salad leaves

FOR THE DRESSING

10ml/2 tsp olive oil
5ml/1 tsp balsamic vinegar
splash of strawberry wine (optional)
salt and ground black pepper

1 Slice the strawberries vertically into three or four pieces, then place in a bowl with the sugar and balsamic vinegar. Leave for 30 minutes.

2 Meanwhile, make the dressing by placing the olive oil and balsamic vinegar in a small bowl and whisking them together with the wine, if you are using it. Add salt and ground black pepper to taste.

3 Cut the smoked venison into little strips. Mix the salad leaves together then toss with the dressing. Distribute the salad leaves among four plates, sprinkle with the strawberries and venison and serve immediately.

COOK'S TIPS
• *Suitable salad leaves include lollo rosso for colour, rocket (arugula) and lamb's lettuce (corn salad) for a peppery flavour, and Little Gem (Bibb) for crunch.*
• *The sugar brings out the moisture in the strawberries, which combines with the balsamic vinegar to create a lovely shiny coat. Do not leave them to stand for too long as they can become limp and tired looking, 30 minutes is about right.*

Nutritional information per portion: Energy 116kcal/486kJ; Protein 11.6g; Carbohydrate 3.1g, of which sugars 3.1g; Fat 6.8g, of which saturates 1.2g; Cholesterol 25mg; Calcium 16mg; Fibre 0.6g; Sodium 31mg.

Side Salads

These salads can refresh the palate, add interest to a main dish and visual appeal to any meal. To serve at a buffet or to accompany grilled meats, Potato Salad with Curry Plant Mayonnaise is a great twist on a popular favourite. Cucumber Salad, with lots of fresh dill, would be perfect with grilled salmon on a summer day. If the main course is pasta, Panzanella is a tasty and colourful salad accompaniment.

Herb salad with chilli and preserved lemon

Firm-leafed fresh herbs, such as flat leaf parsley and mint sautéed in a little olive oil and seasoned with salt, are fabulous to serve as a salad in a meze spread or to accompany spicy kebabs or tagines, or can transform any simple meat or fish into something special.

SERVES 4

a large bunch of flat leaf parsley
a large bunch of mint
a large bunch of fresh coriander (cilantro)
a bunch of rocket (arugula)
a large bunch of spinach leaves
60–75ml/4–5 tbsp olive oil
2 garlic cloves, finely chopped
1 green or red chilli, seeded and
    finely chopped
1/2 preserved lemon, finely chopped
salt and ground black pepper
45–60ml/3–4 tbsp Greek (US strained
    plain) yogurt, to serve

1 Roughly chop the parsley, mint, coriander, rocket and spinach. Heat the olive oil in a wide, heavy pan. Stir in the garlic and chilli, and fry until they begin to colour.

2 Add the herbs, rocket and spinach and cook gently, until soft and wilted. Add the preserved lemon and season. Serve the salad warm with a dollop of yogurt.

MAKING GARLIC-FLAVOURED YOGURT
Crush a clove of garlic and stir it into the yogurt with salt and ground pepper to taste.

Nutritional information per portion: Energy 121kcal/500kJ; Protein 2.3g; Carbohydrate 1.6g, of which sugars 1.4g; Fat 11.8g, of which saturates 1.6g; Cholesterol 0mg; Calcium 128mg; Fibre 2.5g; Sodium 54mg.

Wild rocket and cos lettuce salad

Salads in Greece are clean-tasting and often quite lemony in flavour. The national preference for strong-tasting leaves – sometimes quite bitter ones – is also reflected in fresh salads. Wild rocket is a favourite ingredient, added to give salads a peppery new edge.

SERVES 4

a large handful of rocket (arugula) leaves
2 cos or romaine lettuce hearts
3–4 fresh flat leaf parsley sprigs,
   coarsely chopped
30–45ml/2–3 tbsp finely chopped
   fresh dill
75ml/5 tbsp extra virgin olive oil
15–30ml/1–2 tbsp lemon juice
salt

1 If the rocket leaves are young and tender they can be left whole but older ones should be trimmed of thick stalks and then sliced coarsely.

2 Slice the lettuce in thin ribbons and place these in a bowl, then add the rocket and the chopped parsley and dill.

3 Make a dressing by whisking the oil and lemon juice with salt to taste in a bowl until the mixture emulsifies and thickens. Just before serving, pour over the dressing and toss lightly to coat.

Nutritional information per portion: Energy 134kcal/554kJ; Protein 0.6g; Carbohydrate 1.3g, of which sugars 1.3g; Fat 14.1g, of which saturates 2.1g; Cholesterol 0mg; Calcium 21mg; Fibre 0.7g; Sodium 2mg.

Lamb's lettuce salad

The lamb's lettuce in Turkey is a slightly thicker version of the plant than is generally available elsewhere. Extremely quick and easy, this simple salad can be served as part of a meze spread but is also delicious with grilled and roasted meats and poultry.

SERVES 4

500g/1¼lb Greek (US strained plain) yogurt
juice of 1 lemon
1–2 garlic cloves, crushed
225g/8oz fresh lamb's lettuce, well rinsed and drained
salt and ground black pepper

1 In a wide bowl, beat the yogurt with the lemon juice and garlic. Season to taste with salt and pepper.

2 Toss the lamb's lettuce with the yogurt.

3 Transfer the salad to a serving bowl and serve immediately, while the leaves are still fresh, as a meze dish or as a salad with savoury pastries, or with grilled (broiled) and roasted meats.

Nutritional information per portion: Energy 78kcal/328kJ; Protein 6.8g; Carbohydrate 10.3g, of which sugars 10.3g; Fat 1.5g, of which saturates 0.7g; Cholesterol 2mg; Calcium 253mg; Fibre 0.5g; Sodium 106mg.

COOK'S TIP
Experiment with different ratios of yogurt to lamb's lettuce and make it according to your personal preference. If you do not like garlic, use a herb you like.

Chinese chive and onion salad

This lively salad is a combination of crunchy salad leaves and cabbage with a chilli powder and soy dressing. It is delicious served on its own as a vegetable dish or as a refreshing accompaniment to grilled meat or seafood.

SERVES 2–3

50g/2oz Chinese chives

¼ white onion, finely sliced

1 thin slice red cabbage, finely sliced

1 thin wedge Chinese leaves (Chinese
    cabbage), finely sliced

FOR THE DRESSING

15ml/1 tbsp soy sauce

7.5ml/1½ tbsp Korean chilli powder

7.5ml/1½ tbsp sesame seeds

7.5ml/1½ tbsp sesame oil

5ml/1 tsp cider vinegar

5ml/1 tsp lemon juice

5ml/1 tsp sugar

1 garlic clove, crushed

1 Trim both ends off the Chinese chives and cut them into 5cm/2in long pieces.

2 Soak the onion, and the red cabbage and Chinese leaves, separately in two bowls of iced water for about 5 minutes, to soften the flavours.

3 Drain the onion, cabbage and Chinese leaves, then combine them with the chives in a serving dish and mix thoroughly.

4 For the dressing, combine the soy sauce, chilli powder, sesame seeds and oil, vinegar, lemon juice, sugar and garlic in a bowl. Mix the ingredients and drizzle the dressing over the chive mixture. Serve.

Nutritional information per portion: Energy 47kcal/197kJ; Protein 1.7g; Carbohydrate 6.2g, of which sugars 5.7g; Fat 1.9g, of which saturates 0.3g; Cholesterol 0mg; Calcium 53mg; Fibre 1.8g; Sodium 362mg.

Cucumber salad

Cucumber makes a very refreshing salad. The dressing should be perfectly balanced between sweet and sour, with accents of fresh dill. It is important to make this salad shortly before you intend to serve it, so the cucumber retains its crispness.

SERVES 6

1 large cucumber, about 35cm/14in long
75ml/5 tbsp distilled white vinegar
25g/1oz/2 tbsp sugar
45ml/3 tbsp chopped fresh dill
salt and ground white pepper

1 Cut the cucumber into 3mm/^{1}/$_8$in slices and place in a serving bowl.

2 Combine the vinegar, sugar and dill in a small bowl and season with salt and pepper. Pour the dressing over the cucumber slices and toss to coat evenly. Serve immediately.

COOK'S TIP

This cucumber salad is good served with all kinds of poached fish, especially salmon. The vinegar and sugar can also be mixed into 250ml/8fl oz/1 cup sour cream for a richer, cream-style dressing that goes well with fish cakes and fried fish.

Nutritional information per portion: Energy 30kcal/125kJ; Protein 0.7g; Carbohydrate 1.1g, of which sugars 1g; Fat 2.6g, of which saturates 1.6g; Cholesterol 0mg; Calcium 26mg; Fibre 0.4g; Sodium 8mg.

Cucumber and shallot salad

In Malaysia and Singapore, this light, refreshing salad is served with Indian food almost as often as the cooling mint-flavoured cucumber raita. The Malays also enjoy this salad with many of their spicy fish and grilled meat dishes. It can be made ahead of time and kept in the refrigerator.

SERVES 4

1 cucumber, peeled, halved lengthways and seeded

4 shallots, halved lengthways and sliced finely along the grain

1–2 green chillies, seeded and sliced finely lengthways

60ml/4 tbsp coconut milk

5–10ml/1–2 tsp cumin seeds, dry-roasted and ground to a powder

salt

1 lime, quartered, to serve

1 Slice the cucumber halves finely and sprinkle with salt. Set aside for about 15 minutes. Rinse well and drain off any excess water.

2 Put the cucumber, shallots and chillies in a bowl. Pour in the coconut milk and toss well. Sprinkle most of the roasted cumin over the top. Just before serving, toss the salad again, season with salt, and sprinkle the rest of the roasted cumin over the top. Serve with lime wedges to squeeze over the salad.

Nutritional information per portion: Energy 17Kcal/68kJ; Protein 0.7g; Carbohydrate 3.3g, of which sugars 2.7g; Fat 0.1g, of which saturates 0g; Cholesterol 0mg; Calcium 19mg; Fibre 0.7g; Sodium 15mg.

Lebanese country salad

Each region of the eastern Mediterranean has its own version of a classic salad, which is often said to originate with shepherds, gypsies, travellers or monks or priests. This is a typical, everyday, country salad that can be served with any Lebanese dish, as well as part of a meze spread.

SERVES 4–6

1 cos or romaine lettuce

1 cucumber

2 tomatoes

2–3 spring onions (scallions)

a bunch of fresh mint leaves

a bunch of flat leaf parsley

30ml/2 tbsp olive oil

juice of ¹/₂ lemon

salt

1 Cut the lettuce leaves into bitesize chunks and place in a bowl. Partially peel the cucumber and cut into small chunks, skin the tomatoes and dice the flesh, trim and slice the spring onions and add all the vegetables to the bowl.

2 Wash and finely chop the mint and parsley, discarding the stalks, and add to the vegetables. Toss in the olive oil and lemon juice. Sprinkle with salt and serve.

Nutritional information per portion: Energy 51kcal/210kJ; Protein 1.1g; Carbohydrate 2.5g, of which sugars 2.4g; Fat 4.1g, of which saturates 0.6g; Cholesterol 0mg; Calcium 36mg; Fibre 1.3g; Sodium 8mg.

Summer salad with creamy dressing

Mayonnaise and vinaigrette are not the only dressings for a summer salad. A home-made creamy dressing, such as the one in this recipe, makes a delicious alternative, and tastes much better than store-bought versions.

SERVES 4

2 hard-boiled eggs
15ml/1 tbsp caster (superfine) sugar
2.5ml/¹⁄₂ tsp salt
15ml/1 tbsp Swedish or German mustard
30ml/2 tbsp lemon juice
200ml/7fl oz/scant 1 cup double
    (heavy) cream
summer salad leaves, such as Little
    Gem (Bibb) lettuce
¹⁄₂ cucumber, sliced
15ml/1 tbsp chopped fresh chives or dill

1 Cut the hard-boiled eggs in half, remove the yolks and reserve the whites. Push the yolks through a sieve (strainer) into a bowl, then add the sugar, salt, mustard and lemon juice and blend together.

2 Whisk the cream in a bowl until it begins to thicken but is not stiff. Add to the egg mixture and mix to form a creamy dressing.

3 Arrange the salad leaves and cucumber slices on four individual serving plates and spoon over the dressing. Chop the reserved egg whites and sprinkle over the top with the chopped herbs.

Nutritional information per portion: Energy 315kcal/1302kJ; Protein 4.8g; Carbohydrate 6.7g, of which sugars 6.6g; Fat 30.2g, of which saturates 17.5g; Cholesterol 164mg; Calcium 60mg; Fibre 0.5g; Sodium 405mg.

Ensaladilla

Known as Russian salad elsewhere, this 'salad of little things' became extremely popular during the Spanish Civil War in the 1930s, when more expensive ingredients were scarce.

SERVES 4

8 new potatoes, scrubbed and quartered

1 large carrot, diced

115g/4oz fine green beans, cut into
   2cm/³/₄in lengths

75g/3oz/³/₄ cup peas

¹/₂ Spanish (Bermuda) onion, chopped

4 cornichons or small gherkins, sliced

1 small red (bell) pepper, seeded
   and diced

50g/2oz/¹/₂ cup pitted black olives

15ml/1 tbsp drained pickled capers

15ml/1 tbsp lemon juice

30ml/2 tbsp chopped fresh fennel
   or parsley

salt and ground black pepper

FOR THE AIOLI

2 garlic cloves, finely chopped

2.5ml/¹/₂ tsp salt

150ml/¹/₄ pint/²/₃ cup mayonnaise

1 Make the aioli. Crush the garlic with the salt in a mortar and whisk or stir into the mayonnaise.

2 Cook the potatoes and diced carrot in a pan of boiling lightly salted water for 5–8 minutes until almost tender. Add the beans and peas to the pan and cook for 2 minutes, or until all the vegetables are tender. Drain well.

3 Put the vegetables into a large bowl. Add the onion, cornichons or gherkins, red pepper, olives and

capers. Stir in the aioli and season to taste with pepper and lemon juice.

4 Toss the vegetables and aioli together until well combined, check the seasoning and chill well. Serve garnished with fennel or parsley.

VARIATION

This salad is delicious using any combination of chopped, cooked vegetables. Use whatever is available.

Nutritional information per portion: Energy 494kcal/2045kJ; Protein 5.1g; Carbohydrate 25.6g, of which sugars 8.1g; Fat 42g, of which saturates 6.3g; Cholesterol 28mg; Calcium 60mg; Fibre 4.5g; Sodium 191mg.

Panzanella

In this lively Italian speciality, a sweet tangy blend of tomato juice, rich olive oil and red wine vinegar is soaked up in a colourful salad of roasted peppers, anchovies and toasted ciabatta.

SERVES 4–6

225g/8oz ciabatta (about ²/₃ loaf)
150ml/¼ pint/²/₃ cup olive oil
3 red (bell) peppers
3 yellow (bell) peppers
50g/2oz can anchovy fillets
675g/1½lb ripe plum tomatoes
4 garlic cloves, crushed
60ml/4 tbsp red wine vinegar
50g/2oz capers
115g/4oz/1 cup pitted black olives
salt and ground black pepper
basil leaves, to garnish

1 Preheat the oven to 200°C/400°F/ Gas 6. Cut the ciabatta into 2cm/³/₄in chunks and drizzle with 50ml/2fl oz/¼ cup of the oil. Grill (broil) lightly until just golden.

2 Bake the peppers for about 45 minutes until the skin begins to char. Remove from the oven, cover with a cloth and leave to cool slightly.

3 Pull the skin off the peppers and cut them into quarters, discarding the stalk ends and seeds. Drain and chop the anchovies. Set aside.

4 Peel and halve the tomatoes. Scoop the seeds into a sieve set over a bowl. Using the back of a spoon, press the tomato pulp in the sieve (strainer) to extract as much juice as possible. Discard the pulp and add the remaining oil, the garlic and vinegar to the juices.

5 Layer the ciabatta, peppers, tomatoes, anchovies, capers and olives in a bowl. Season the tomato dressing with salt and pepper and pour it over the salad. Stand for 30 minutes. Serve garnished with basil.

Nutritional information per portion: Energy 360kcal/1500kJ; Protein 8.6g; Carbohydrate 33.7g, of which sugars 14.8g; Fat 22.1g, of which saturates 3.3g; Cholesterol 5mg; Calcium 103mg; Fibre 5.2g; Sodium 977mg.

Roasted peppers with tomatoes

This Mediterranean-style dish is a real treat. If you make and dress this salad an hour or two before serving, the juices mingle and the flavours are intensified.

SERVES 4

1 red (bell) pepper
1 yellow (bell) pepper
4 ripe plum tomatoes, sliced
2 canned artichokes, drained
    and quartered
4 sun-dried tomatoes in oil, drained and
    thinly sliced
15ml/1 tbsp capers, drained
1 garlic clove, sliced
a few basil leaves, to garnish

FOR THE DRESSING
15ml/1 tbsp balsamic vinegar
5ml/1 tsp lemon juice
75ml/5 tbsp extra virgin olive oil
15ml/1 tbsp chopped fresh parsley
    and chives
salt and ground black pepper

1 Cut the peppers in half, and remove the seeds and stalks. Cut into quarters and place on a grill (broiler) pan covered with foil. Cook, skin side up, under a grill (broiler) set on high, until the skin chars. Transfer to a bowl and cover. Leave the peppers to cool.

2 Rub the skin off the peppers, remove the seeds and cores, then cut them into strips.

3 Arrange the pepper strips, plum tomatoes and canned artichokes on a serving dish. Sprinkle over the sun-dried tomatoes, capers and garlic.

4 To make the dressing, put the balsamic vinegar and lemon juice in a bowl and whisk in the olive oil, then the chopped herbs. Season with salt and pepper. Pour the dressing over the salad 1–2 hours before the salad is served, if possible. Serve, garnished with basil leaves.

Nutritional information per portion: Energy 216kcal/890kJ; Protein 1.5g; Carbohydrate 8.1g, of which sugars 7.9g; Fat 19.9g, of which saturates 2.9g; Cholesterol 0mg; Calcium 22mg; Fibre 2.4g; Sodium 24mg.

Tricolour salad

A popular salad, this dish depends for success on the quality of its ingredients. Mozzarella is the best cheese to serve uncooked, and ripe plum tomatoes are essential.

SERVES 2–3

150g/5oz mozzarella, thinly sliced

4 large plum tomatoes, sliced

1 large avocado

about 12 basil leaves or a small handful
of flat leaf parsley leaves

45–60ml/3–4 tbsp extra virgin olive oil

sea salt flakes and ground black pepper

ciabatta, to serve

1 Arrange the sliced mozzarella cheese and tomatoes randomly on two salad plates. Crush over a few good pinches of sea salt flakes. This will help to draw out some of the juices from the plum tomatoes. Set aside in a cool place and leave to marinate for about 30 minutes.

2 Just before serving, cut the avocado in half using a sharp knife and twist the halves to separate. Lift out the stone (pit) and remove the peel.

3 Carefully slice the avocado flesh crossways into half moons, or cut it into large chunks if that is easier.

4 Place the avocado on the salad, then sprinkle with the basil or parsley. Drizzle over the olive oil, add a little more salt if needed and some black pepper.

5 Serve at room temperature, with chunks of crusty Italian ciabatta for mopping up the dressing.

Nutritional information per portion: Energy 526kcal/2180kJ; Protein 17.5g; Carbohydrate 8.3g, of which sugars 7.2g; Fat 47.1g, of which saturates 16g; Cholesterol 44mg; Calcium 344mg; Fibre 5.8g; Sodium 327mg.

Raw vegetable yam

In this context, the word 'yam' does not refer to the starchy vegetable that resembles sweet potato, but rather to a unique style of Thai cooking. Yam dishes are salads made with raw or lightly cooked vegetables, dressed with a special spicy sauce.

SERVES 4

50g/2oz watercress or baby spinach, chopped
1/2 cucumber, finely diced
2 celery sticks, finely diced
2 carrots, finely diced
1 red (bell) pepper, seeded and finely diced
2 tomatoes, seeded and finely diced
a small bunch of fresh mint, chopped
90g/3½oz cellophane noodles

FOR THE YAM
2 small fresh red chillies, seeded and
    finely chopped
60ml/4 tbsp light soy sauce

45ml/3 tbsp lemon juice
5ml/1 tsp palm sugar (jaggery) or
    light muscovado (brown) sugar
60ml/4 tbsp water
1 head pickled garlic, finely chopped,
    plus 15ml/1 tbsp vinegar from the jar
50g/2oz/scant 1/2 cup peanuts, roasted
    and chopped
90g/3½oz fried tofu, finely chopped
15ml/1 tbsp sesame seeds, toasted

1 Place the watercress or spinach, cucumber, celery, carrots, red pepper and tomatoes in a bowl. Add the chopped mint and toss together.

2 Soak the noodles in boiling water for 3 minutes, or according to the packet instructions, then drain well and snip with scissors into shorter lengths. Add them to the vegetables.

3 Make the yam. Put the chopped chillies in a pan and add the soy sauce, lemon juice, sugar and water. Place over a medium heat and stir until the sugar has dissolved.

4 Add the garlic to the pan, with the pickling vinegar from the jar, then mix in the chopped peanuts, tofu and toasted sesame seeds.

5 Pour the yam over the vegetables and noodles, toss together until well mixed, and serve immediately.

Nutritional information per portion: Energy 490kcal/2043kJ; Protein 18.9g; Carbohydrate 28.5g, of which sugars 21g; Fat 34.3g, of which saturates 8.6g; Cholesterol 0mg; Calcium 80mg; Fibre 6.2g; Sodium 493mg.

Coleslaw with blue cheese

In this dish, shredded crisp white cabbage is tossed in a dressing flavoured with English blue cheese. Serve it with other salads or with hot potatoes baked in their skins.

SERVES 4–8

45ml/3 tbsp mayonnaise

45ml/3 tbsp thick natural (plain) yogurt

50g/2oz blue cheese, such as Stilton or
   Oxford Blue, crumbled

15ml/1 tbsp lemon juice

500g/1¼lb white cabbage

1 medium carrot

1 small red onion

2 small celery sticks

1 crisp eating apple

salt and ground black pepper

watercress or parsley sprigs, to garnish

1 To make the dressing, put the mayonnaise and yogurt into a bowl and add the cheese. Stir, adding lemon juice and seasoning to taste.

2 Trim and shred the cabbage finely, grate the carrot, chop the onion finely and cut the celery into very thin slices. Core and dice the apple.

3 Add the cabbage, carrot, onion, celery and apple to the bowl and toss until all the ingredients are well mixed and coated with the dressing.

4 Cover the bowl and chill for 2–3 hours or until ready to serve. Stir before serving, and garnish with watercress or parsley.

Nutritional information per portion: Energy 86kcal/359kJ; Protein 2.7g; Carbohydrate 5.1g, of which sugars 4.8g; Fat 6.3g, of which saturates 1.9g; Cholesterol 9mg; Calcium 78mg; Fibre 1.6g; Sodium 116mg.

Cabbage salad

This is a simple and delicious way of serving a somewhat mundane vegetable. Classic Thai flavours permeate this colourful warm salad.

SERVES 4–6

30ml/2 tbsp vegetable oil

2 large fresh red chillies, seeded and cut
   into thin strips

6 garlic cloves, thinly sliced

6 shallots, thinly sliced

1 small cabbage, shredded

30ml/2 tbsp coarsely chopped roasted
   peanuts, to garnish

FOR THE DRESSING

30ml/2 tbsp Thai fish sauce

grated rind of 1 lime

30ml/2 tbsp lime juice

120ml/4fl oz/¹/₂ cup coconut milk

1 Make the dressing by mixing the fish sauce, lime rind and juice and coconut milk in a bowl. Whisk until thoroughly combined. Set aside.

2 Heat the oil in a wok. Stir-fry the chillies, garlic and shallots over a medium heat for 3–4 minutes, until the shallots are brown and crisp. Remove from the wok with a slotted spoon and set aside.

3 Bring a large pan of lightly salted water to the boil. Add the cabbage and blanch for 2–3 minutes. Drain it well in a sieve (strainer) or colander, then transfer to a bowl.

4 Whisk the dressing again, add to the warm cabbage and toss to mix. Transfer to a serving dish. Sprinkle with the fried shallot mixture and the peanuts. Serve immediately.

Nutritional information per portion: Energy 124kcal/513kJ; Protein 3.4g; Carbohydrate 7.1g, of which sugars 6.5g; Fat 9.2g, of which saturates 1.4g; Cholesterol 0mg; Calcium 57mg; Fibre 2.3g; Sodium 306mg.

Cabbage salad with lemon vinaigrette and olives

This Greek salad, which has a crisp and refreshing texture, is made with compact creamy-coloured "white" cabbage. As a variation, green olives and chives could be used.

SERVES 4

1 white cabbage
12 black olives

FOR THE VINAIGRETTE
75–90ml/5–6 tbsp extra virgin olive oil
30ml/2 tbsp lemon juice
1 garlic clove, crushed
30ml/2 tbsp finely chopped fresh flat
    leaf parsley
salt

1 Cut the cabbage in quarters, discard the outer leaves and trim off any thick, hard stems as well as the hard base.

2 Lay each quarter in turn on its side and cut long, very thin slices until you reach the central core, which should be discarded. The key to a perfect cabbage salad is to shred the cabbage as finely as possible. Place the shredded cabbage in a bowl and stir in the black olives.

3 Make the vinaigrette by whisking the olive oil, lemon juice, garlic, parsley and salt together in a bowl until well blended. Pour the dressing over the salad, and toss the cabbage and olives until the cabbage and olives are evenly coated.

Nutritional information per portion: Energy 307kcal/1269kJ; Protein 3.9g; Carbohydrate 12.8g, of which sugars 12.5g; Fat 26.9g, of which saturates 3.8g; Cholesterol 0mg; Calcium 145mg; Fibre 5.8g; Sodium 21mg.

Hot and sour noodle salad

Noodles make the perfect basis for a salad, absorbing the dressing and providing the ideal contrast in texture to the crisp vegetables.

SERVES 2

200g/7oz thin rice noodles
a small bunch of fresh coriander
(cilantro)
2 tomatoes, seeded and sliced
130g/4¹/₂oz baby corn cobs, sliced
4 spring onions (scallions), thinly sliced
1 red (bell) pepper, seeded and chopped
juice of 2 limes
2 small fresh green chillies, seeded
and chopped
10ml/2 tsp sugar
115g/4oz/1 cup peanuts, toasted
and chopped
30ml/2 tbsp soy sauce
salt

1 Bring a pan of lightly salted water to the boil. Snap the noodles into short lengths, add to the pan and cook for 3–4 minutes. Drain, rinse under cold water and drain again.

2 Set aside a few coriander leaves for the garnish. Chop the remaining leaves and place them in a large serving bowl.

3 Add the noodles to the bowl, with the tomato slices, corn cobs, spring onions, red pepper, lime juice, chillies, sugar and chopped peanuts. Season with the soy sauce, then taste and add a little salt if you think the mixture needs it. Toss the salad lightly but thoroughly, then garnish with the reserved coriander leaves and serve immediately.

Nutritional information per portion: Energy 412kcal/1721kJ; Protein 13g; Carbohydrate 56g, of which sugars 10.7g; Fat 14.7g, of which saturates 2.8g; Cholesterol 0mg; Calcium 68mg; Fibre 4.5g; Sodium 971mg.

Malay beansprout salad

This beansprout salad is often served as a refreshing side dish to accompany a famous dish known as 'blue rice' and other highly spiced Malay dishes.

SERVES 4

115g/4oz fresh coconut, grated

30ml/2 tbsp dried prawns (shrimp)

225g/8oz beansprouts, rinsed and drained

1 small cucumber, peeled, seeded and cut
   into julienne strips

2–3 spring onions (scallions), trimmed,
   cut into 2.5cm/1in pieces and
   halved lengthways

50g/2oz young, tender mangetouts
   (snow peas), halved diagonally

50g/2oz green beans, halved lengthways

a handful of fresh chives, chopped

a handful of fresh mint leaves,
   finely chopped

2–3 red chillies, seeded and sliced
   finely lengthways

juice of 2 limes

10ml/2 tsp sugar

salt and ground black pepper

1 Dry-roast the grated coconut in a heavy frying pan until it starts to emit a nutty aroma and is lightly browned but not burnt. Using a mortar and pestle or a food processor, grind the coconut to a coarse powder. Soak the dried prawns for about 1 hour or until they are soft, then drain and grind them coarsely.

2 Put the vegetables, herbs and chillies into a bowl. Mix the lime juice with the sugar and pour it over the salad. Season with salt and pepper. Sprinkle the ground coconut and dried prawns over the salad, and toss well until thoroughly mixed.

COOK'S TIP

Aim to cut all the vegetables into thin strips that are about the same size and shape as the beansprouts.

Nutritional information per portion: Energy 230kcal/947kJ; Protein 12.6g; Carbohydrate 15.9g, of which sugars 13.9g; Fat 12.9g, of which saturates 10.2g; Cholesterol 0mg; Calcium 151mg; Fibre 7.8g; Sodium 24mg.

Bamboo shoot salad

This hot, sharp-flavoured salad originated in north-eastern Thailand. Use canned whole bamboo shoots, if you can find them – they have more flavour than sliced ones.

SERVES 4

400g/14oz canned bamboo shoots
25g/1oz glutinous rice
30ml/2 tbsp chopped shallots
15ml/1 tbsp chopped garlic
45ml/3 tbsp chopped spring
    onions (scallions)
30ml/2 tbsp Thai fish sauce
30ml/2 tbsp fresh lime juice
5ml/1 tsp sugar
2.5ml/¹/₂ tsp dried chilli flakes
20–25 small fresh mint leaves
15ml/1 tbsp toasted sesame seeds

1 Rinse the bamboo shoots under cold running water, then drain them and pat them thoroughly dry with kitchen paper. Cut them into large pieces, or leave them whole, and set them aside.

2 Dry-roast the rice in a frying pan until golden brown. Leave to cool slightly, then place in a mortar and grind to fine crumbs with a pestle.

3 Transfer the rice to a bowl and add the shallots, garlic, spring onions, fish sauce, lime juice, sugar, chillies and half the mint leaves. Mix well.

4 Add the bamboo shoots to the bowl and toss to mix. Serve sprinkled with toasted sesame seeds and the remaining mint leaves.

Nutritional information per portion: Energy 80kcal/336kJ; Protein 4.5g; Carbohydrate 9.4g, of which sugars 2.9g; Fat 2.8g, of which saturates 0.4g; Cholesterol 0mg; Calcium 51mg; Fibre 2g; Sodium 185mg.

Gypsy salad with feta, chillies and parsley

In Turkey, this salad is often eaten as meze, or served as an accompaniment to meat and fish dishes. It is called çingene pilavı, *meaning 'gypsy rice'. A chilli is included to give a kick, and crumbled feta is added to represent the rice.*

SERVES 3–4

2 red onions, cut in half lengthways and
    finely sliced along the grain
1 green (bell) pepper, seeded and sliced
1 fresh green chilli, seeded and chopped
2–3 garlic cloves, chopped
a bunch of fresh flat leaf parsley, chopped
225g/8oz firm feta cheese, rinsed and
    grated
2 large tomatoes, skinned, seeded and
    finely chopped
30–45ml/2–3 tbsp olive oil
salt and ground black pepper

TO SERVE
scant 5ml/1 tsp Turkish red pepper flakes
    or paprika
scant 5ml/1 tsp ground sumac

1 Sprinkle the onions with a little salt to draw out the juice. Leave for about 10 minutes, then rinse and pat dry.

2 Put the onions and green pepper in a bowl with the chilli, garlic, parsley, feta and tomatoes.

3 Add the oil and seasoning and toss well.

4 Transfer the salad to a large serving dish and sprinkle with the red pepper or paprika and sumac.

Nutritional information per portion: Energy 253kcal/1049kJ; Protein 11.1g; Carbohydrate 13.4g, of which sugars 11g; Fat 17.6g, of which saturates 8.6g; Cholesterol 39mg; Calcium 260mg; Fibre 3.2g; Sodium 824mg.

Blue cheese and walnut salad

Any blue cheese with a creamy texture and tangy flavour will be ideal for this piquant salad. It makes a delicious fresh-tasting first course but it could be served without the figs as an interesting cheese course.

SERVES 4

225g/8oz mixed salad leaves

4 fresh figs

115g/4oz blue cheese, such as Roquefort, cut into small chunks

75g/3oz/³/₄ cup walnuts, broken in pieces

FOR THE DRESSING

45ml/3 tbsp walnut oil

juice of 1 lemon

salt and ground black pepper

1 Mix all the dressing ingredients together in a bowl. Whisk briskly until thick and emulsified.

2 Wash and dry the salad leaves then tear them gently into bitesize pieces. Place in a mixing bowl and toss with the dressing. Transfer to a large serving dish or divide among four individual plates, ensuring a good balance of colour and texture on each plate.

3 Cut the figs into quarters and add to the salad leaves.

4 Sprinkle the cheese over, crumbling it slightly. Then sprinkle over the walnuts, and serve immediately.

Nutritional information per portion: Energy 415kcal/1726kJ; Protein 10.6g; Carbohydrate 26.6g, of which sugars 26.4g; Fat 30.3g, of which saturates 7.3g; Cholesterol 22mg; Calcium 286mg; Fibre 4.5g; Sodium 383mg.

Sweet and sour artichoke salad

Agrodolce is a sweet and sour sauce which works perfectly in this salad. 'Agro' means 'sour' and 'dolce' means 'sweet'.

SERVES 4

6 small globe artichokes
juice of 1 lemon
30ml/2 tbsp olive oil
2 medium onions, roughly chopped
175g/6oz/1 cup fresh or frozen broad
   (fava) beans (shelled weight)
175g/6oz/1½ cups fresh or frozen peas
   (shelled weight)
salt and freshly ground black pepper
fresh mint leaves, to garnish

FOR THE SALSA AGRODOLCE
120ml/4fl oz/½ cup white wine vinegar
15ml/1 tbsp caster (superfine) sugar
handful fresh mint leaves, roughly torn

1 Peel the outer leaves from the artichokes and cut into quarters. Place the artichokes in a bowl of water with the lemon juice.

2 Heat the oil in a large pan and add the onions. Cook until the onions are golden. Add the beans and stir, then drain the artichokes and add to the pan. Pour in 300ml/ ½ pint/1¼ cups of water and cook, covered, for 10–15 minutes.

3 Add the peas, season with salt and pepper and cook for a further 5 minutes, stirring from time to time, until the vegetables are tender. Drain in a sieve (strainer) and place all the vegetables in a bowl, leave to cool, then cover and chill.

4 To make the salsa agrodolce, mix all the ingredients in a small pan. Heat gently for 2–3 minutes until the sugar has dissolved. Simmer gently for about 5 minutes, stirring occasionally. Leave to cool. To serve, drizzle the salsa agrodolce over the vegetables and garnish with mint leaves.

Nutritional information per portion: Energy 172kcal/717kJ; Protein 8g; Carbohydrate 21g, of which sugars 10.8g; Fat 6.8g, of which saturates 1g; Cholesterol 0mg; Calcium 106mg; Fibre 7.3g; Sodium 82mg.

Artichokes with garlic, lemon and olive oil

This classic dish of Florence is said to be of Jewish origin. It is not only delicious as a salad on its own, but can also accompany roasted fish, chicken or lamb dishes.

SERVES 4

4 globe artichokes

juice of 1–2 lemons, plus 15ml/1 tbsp extra to acidulate water

60ml/4 tbsp extra virgin olive oil

1 onion, chopped

5–8 garlic cloves, roughly chopped or thinly sliced

30ml/2 tbsp chopped fresh parsley

120ml/4fl oz/½ cup dry white wine

120ml/4fl oz/½ cup vegetable stock or water

salt and ground black pepper

1 Prepare the artichokes. Pull back and remove the tough leaves. Peel the tender part of the stems and cut into bitesize pieces, then put in a bowl of acidulated water. Cut the artichokes into quarters and cut out the thistle heart. Add to the bowl.

2 Heat the oil in a pan, add the onion and garlic and fry for 5 minutes until softened. Stir in the parsley and cook for a few seconds. Add the wine, stock or water and drained artichokes. Season with half the lemon juice, salt and pepper.

3 Bring the mixture to the boil, then lower the heat, cover and simmer for 10–15 minutes until the artichokes are just tender. Lift them out with a slotted spoon and transfer them to a serving dish.

4 Bring the cooking liquid to the boil and boil until reduced to about half its volume. Pour the mixture over the artichokes and drizzle with the remaining lemon juice. Taste for seasoning and cool before serving.

Nutritional information per portion: Energy 142kcal/586kJ; Protein 1.6g; Carbohydrate 4.1g, of which sugars 1.9g; Fat 11.3g, of which saturates 1.6g; Cholesterol 0mg; Calcium 40mg; Fibre 1.6g; Sodium 47mg.

Grated beetroot and yogurt salad

With its beneficial nutritional properties, yogurt is used frequently in meze dishes. In this recipe it is added to a tasty salad of grated, cooked beetroot, and mixed with some shredded mint leaves. Spiked with garlic and a pretty shade of pink, it is very moreish scooped on to flat bread.

SERVES 4

4 raw beetroot (beets), washed
    and trimmed
500ml/17fl oz/generous 2 cups thick and
    creamy natural (plain) yogurt
2 garlic cloves, crushed
salt and ground black pepper
a few fresh mint leaves, shredded,
    to garnish

1 Boil the beetroot in plenty of water for 35–40 minutes until tender, but not mushy or soft. Drain and refresh under cold running water, then peel off the skins and grate the beetroot on to a plate. Squeeze it lightly with your fingers to drain off excess water.

2 In a bowl, beat the yogurt with the garlic and season with salt and pepper. Add the beetroot, reserving a little to garnish the top, and mix well. Garnish with mint leaves and the reserved beetroot.

A CARROT VERSION

Cut four carrots into chunks and steam for about 15 minutes, until they are tender but still with some bite, then grate and mix with the yogurt and garlic. Season with salt and pepper and garnish with mint or dill.

Nutritional information per portion: Energy 95kcal/403kJ; Protein 7.8g; Carbohydrate 14.4g, of which sugars 13g; Fat 1.4g, of which saturates 0.6g; Cholesterol 2mg; Calcium 249mg; Fibre 1.3g; Sodium 137mg.

Christmas beetroot, apple and potato salad

This salad is part of the traditional Christmas table and it is Finland's equivalent of the Swedish smörgåsbord or Russian zakouski. It is traditionally served on Christmas Eve, just as the festive excitement begins to mount.

SERVES 4

1 eating apple
3 cooked potatoes, finely diced
2 large gherkins, finely diced
3 cooked beetroot (beets), finely diced
3 cooked carrots, finely diced
1 onion, finely chopped
500ml/17fl oz/generous 2 cups double
   (heavy) cream
3 hard-boiled eggs, roughly chopped
15ml/1 tbsp chopped fresh parsley
salt and ground white pepper

1 Cut the apple into small dice. Put in a bowl and add the potatoes, gherkins, beetroot, carrots and onion and season with salt and pepper. Carefully mix together and spoon into individual serving glasses or bowls.

2 Mix any beetroot juice into the cream to flavour and give it a pinkish colour, then spoon over the vegetables and apple. Sprinkle the chopped eggs and parsley on top before serving.

VARIATION
Stir in 1/2 finely chopped salted herring fillet or 2 finely chopped anchovy fillets to the mixture with the parsley to add an extra dimension to the dish. Omit the added salt.

Nutritional information per portion: Energy 717kcal/2959kJ; Protein 8.5g; Carbohydrate 11g, of which sugars 10.2g; Fat 71.5g, of which saturates 42.9g; Cholesterol 314mg; Calcium 114mg; Fibre 2.3g; Sodium 132mg.

Celery and coconut salad with lime

This salad is served in Turkey, where it is unusual for its use of grated coconut, which is mainly reserved as a garnish for sweet dishes. Juicy and refreshing, it is welcome on a hot sunny day as part of a buffet, or to accompany grilled meats and spicy dishes.

SERVES 3–4

45–60ml/3–4 tbsp thick and creamy natural (plain) yogurt
2 garlic cloves, crushed
5ml/1 tsp grated lime rind
juice of 1 lime

8 long celery sticks, grated (leaves reserved for the garnish)
flesh of 1/2 fresh coconut, grated
salt and ground black pepper
a few sprigs of fresh flat leaf parsley, to garnish

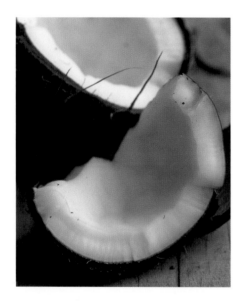

1 Mix the yogurt and garlic in a bowl, add the lime rind and juice and season with salt and pepper.

2 Fold in the grated celery and coconut, then set aside for 15–20 minutes to let the celery juices weep. Don't leave it for too long or it will become watery.

3 To serve, spoon the salad into a bowl and garnish with the celery leaves and flat leaf parsley.

TO MAKE MEDIEVAL MEZE
In some old-fashioned drinking haunts in Istanbul, you can still find the refreshing medieval dish of gleaming, ruby red pomegranate seeds tossed with fine shavings of fresh coconut and a squeeze of lemon or lime – a delight to the eye and palate.

Nutritional information per portion: Energy 126kcal/521kJ; Protein 2.1g; Carbohydrate 2.9g, of which sugars 2.9g; Fat 11.9g, of which saturates 10.1g; Cholesterol 0mg; Calcium 63mg; Fibre 3.6g; Sodium 69mg.

Bean salad with garlic and coriander

This traditional salad is popular as a meze dish but it is also served as an accompaniment to grilled meats. It is always made when fresh broad beans are in season but it is also very good when prepared with frozen beans.

SERVES 4–6

500g/1¼lb/3½ cups shelled broad
   (fava) beans
5ml/1 tsp sugar
30–45ml/2–3 tbsp olive oil
juice of ½ lemon
1–2 cloves garlic, crushed
salt and ground black pepper
small bunch of fresh coriander (cilantro),
   finely chopped

1 Put the shelled beans in a pan with just enough water to cover. Stir in the sugar to preserve the colour of the beans, and bring the water to the boil. Reduce the heat and simmer, uncovered, for about 15 minutes, until the beans are cooked but remain al dente.

2 Drain the beans and refresh them under running cold water, then drain again and put them in a serving bowl.

3 In a bowl, whisk together the oil, lemon juice and garlic. Season well with salt and pepper to taste, and stir in the coriander.

4 Pour the dressing over the beans and toss well to mix. Place the salad in the refrigerator if not serving immediately.

Nutritional information per portion: Energy 111kcal/464kJ; Protein 6.8g; Carbohydrate 10.7g, of which sugars 2g; Fat 4.8g, of which saturates 0.7g; Cholesterol 0mg; Calcium 64mg; Fibre 5.8g; Sodium 10mg.

Potato salad

While the potato is now a staple on Danish tables, it wasn't always that way. Though it reached Europe in 1570, the hardy tuber didn't arrive in Denmark until almost two centuries later. Today, a meal there always includes some form of potatoes, and cold potato salad is a favourite.

SERVES 6–8

1.8kg/4lb potatoes
45ml/3 tbsp finely chopped onion
2 celery stalks, finely chopped
250ml/8fl oz/1 cup sour cream
250ml/8fl oz/1 cup mayonnaise
5ml/1 tsp mustard powder
4ml/¾ tsp celery seed
75ml/5 tbsp chopped fresh dill
salt and ground white pepper

1 Boil the potatoes in lightly salted water for 20–25 minutes, until tender, then drain and allow to cool. Peel and coarsely chop the potatoes and place them in a large mixing bowl. Add the onion and celery.

2 Make the dressing: in a separate bowl, stir together the sour cream, mayonnaise, mustard, celery seed, dill, salt and pepper.

3 Add the dressing to the potatoes and toss gently to coat evenly with the dressing. Adjust the seasoning, cover the bowl and chill until ready to serve.

VARIATIONS
Add chopped cucumber, crumbled crisp bacon, or chopped hard-boiled eggs to the potato salad.

Nutritional information per portion: Energy 440kcal/1834kJ; Protein 5.2g; Carbohydrate 38.5g, of which sugars 4.9g; Fat 30.5g, of which saturates 7.7g; Cholesterol 42mg; Calcium 50mg; Fibre 2.4g; Sodium 183mg.

Potato salad with curry plant mayonnaise

Potato salad can be made well in advance and is therefore a useful dish for serving as part of a menu for entertaining. Its popularity means that there are very rarely any leftovers.

SERVES 6

1kg/2¼lb new potatoes, in skins
300ml/½ pint/1¼ cups home-made or
    bought mayonnaise
6 curry plant leaves, roughly chopped
salt and ground black pepper
mixed lettuce leaves or other salad
    leaves, to serve

1 Place the potatoes in a pan of salted water, bring to the boil and cook for 15 minutes or until tender. Drain and place in a large bowl to cool slightly.

2 Mix the mayonnaise with the curry plant leaves and black pepper, and stir into the potatoes while they are still warm. Cool, then serve on a bed of lettuce leaves or other leaves.

Nutritional information per portion: Energy 474kcal/1967kJ; Protein 4.1g; Carbohydrate 29.1g, of which sugars 4.2g; Fat 38.7g, of which saturates 6g; Cholesterol 38mg; Calcium 37mg; Fibre 2.4g; Sodium 246mg.

Tunisienne potato and olive salad

This delicious salad is favoured in North Africa. It is simple, yet full of interesting flavours.
Serve for lunch as an accompaniment or as an appetizer.

SERVES 4

8 large new potatoes

large pinch of salt

large pinch of sugar

3 garlic cloves, chopped

15ml/1 tbsp vinegar of your choice, such
as a fruit variety

large pinch of ground cumin or whole
cumin seeds

pinch of cayenne pepper or hot paprika,
to taste

30–45ml/2–3 tbsp extra virgin olive oil

30–45ml/2–3 tbsp chopped fresh
coriander (cilantro) leaves

10–15 dry-fleshed black
Mediterranean olives

1 Chop the new potatoes into chunks. Put them in a pan, pour in water to cover and add the salt and sugar. Bring to the boil, then reduce the heat and boil gently for about 10 minutes, or until the potatoes are just tender. Drain well and leave in a colander to cool.

2 When cool enough to handle, slice the potatoes and put in a bowl.

3 Mix the garlic, vinegar, cumin and cayenne or paprika, and pour over the salad. Drizzle with olive oil and sprinkle over the coriander and olives. Chill before serving.

Nutritional information per portion: Energy 375kcal/1581kJ; Protein 7.1g; Carbohydrate 64.5g, of which sugars 5.3g; Fat 11.6g, of which saturates 1.9g; Cholesterol 0mg; Calcium 43mg; Fibre 4.7g; Sodium 467mg.

Caribbean potato salad

Colourful vegetables in a creamy smooth dressing make this piquant Caribbean salad ideal to serve on its own or with grilled or cold meats.

SERVES 6

900g/2lb small waxy or salad potatoes
2 red (bell) peppers, seeded and diced
2 celery sticks, finely chopped
1 shallot, finely chopped
2–3 spring onions (scallions),
    finely chopped
1 mild fresh green chilli, seeded and
    finely chopped
1 garlic clove, crushed
10ml/2 tsp finely chopped chives
10ml/2 tsp finely chopped basil
15ml/1 tbsp finely chopped parsley
15ml/1 tbsp single (light) cream
30ml/2 tbsp salad cream
15ml/1 tbsp mayonnaise
5ml/1 tsp Dijon mustard
7.5ml/¹/₂ tbsp sugar
chopped chives, to garnish
chopped red chilli, to garnish

1 Cook the potatoes in a large saucepan of boiling water until tender but still firm. Drain and leave to one side. When cool enough to handle, cut the cooked potatoes into 2.5cm/1in cubes and place in a large salad bowl.

2 Add all the vegetables to the potatoes in the salad bowl, together with the chopped chilli, crushed garlic and all the chopped herbs.

3 Mix together the cream, salad cream, mayonnaise, mustard and sugar in a small bowl. Stir well until the mixture is thoroughly combined and forms a smooth dressing.

4 Pour the dressing over the potato mixture and stir gently to coat evenly. Serve immediately, garnished with the chopped chives and red chilli.

Nutritional information per portion: Energy 176kcal/743kJ; Protein 3.8g; Carbohydrate 31.3g, of which sugars 8.7g; Fat 4.8g, of which saturates 1g; Cholesterol 5mg; Calcium 42mg; Fibre 3.2g; Sodium 92mg.

Aubergine with walnuts and pomegranate seeds

Variations of this excellent salad can be found throughout the eastern Mediterranean. Serve it either warm or at room temperature to enjoy the subtle, smoky flavour of the aubergine.

SERVES 4–6

2 aubergines (eggplants)
2 tomatoes, skinned, seeded and chopped
1 green (bell) pepper, chopped
1 red onion, finely chopped
a bunch of flat leaf parsley,
   finely chopped
2 cloves garlic, crushed
30–45ml/2–3 tbsp olive oil
juice of 1 lemon
15–30ml/1–2 tbsp walnuts,
   finely chopped
15–30ml/1–2 tbsp pomegranate seeds
salt and ground black pepper

1 Place the aubergines on a hot ridged griddle, or directly over a gas flame or a charcoal grill, and leave to char until soft, turning them from time to time. Hold the aubergines by their stems under running cold water and peel off the charred skins, or slit open the skins and scoop out the flesh.

2 Squeeze out the excess water from the aubergine flesh then chop it to a pulp and place it in a bowl with the tomatoes, pepper, onion, parsley and garlic. Add the olive oil and lemon juice and toss thoroughly. Season to taste with salt and pepper, then stir in half the walnuts and pomegranate seeds.

3 Turn the salad into a serving dish and garnish with the remaining walnuts and pomegranate seeds.

Nutritional information per portion: Energy 90kcal/374kJ; Protein 2.2g; Carbohydrate 7.3g, of which sugars 6.3g; Fat 6g, of which saturates 0.8g; Cholesterol 0mg; Calcium 39mg; Fibre 3.1g; Sodium 10mg.

Pumpkin salad

Red wine vinegar brings out the sweetness of the pumpkin. No salad leaves are used, just plenty of fresh parsley. Eaten throughout Latin America, it is great for a cold buffet.

SERVES 4

1 large red onion, peeled and very
   thinly sliced
200ml/7fl oz/scant 1 cup olive oil
60ml/4 tbsp red wine vinegar
675g/1¹⁄₂lb pumpkin, peeled and cut into
   4cm/1¹⁄₂in pieces
40g/1¹⁄₂oz/³⁄₄ cup fresh flat leaf parsley
   leaves, chopped
salt and ground black pepper

1 Mix the onion, olive oil and vinegar in a large bowl. Stir well to combine.

2 Put the pumpkin in a large pan of cold salted water. Bring to the boil, then lower the heat and simmer gently for 15–20 minutes until tender. Drain.

3 Immediately add the drained, hot pumpkin to the bowl containing the dressing and toss lightly with your hands. Leave to cool. Stir in the chopped parsley, cover with clear film (plastic wrap) and chill. Allow the salad to come back to room temperature before serving.

VARIATIONS
Try replacing the pumpkin with sweet potatoes. Wild rocket (arugula) or fresh coriander (cilantro) can be used instead of the parsley, if you prefer.

Nutritional information per portion: Energy 223kcal/939kJ; Protein 6.9g; Carbohydrate 48.1g, of which sugars 15.9g; Fat 1.5g, of which saturates 0.2g; Cholesterol 0mg; Calcium 61mg; Fibre 2.9g; Sodium 35mg.

Toasted bread salad with sumac

This is one of the classic Lebanese dishes that were devised to make use of leftover bread. Sumac, the deep red, fruity spice from the Middle East, is an essential component.

SERVES 4–6

1–2 flat breads, such as pitta breads
¹/₂ cos or romaine lettuce
2–3 tomatoes, skinned
1 carrot, peeled
5–6 small radishes
1 red or green (bell) pepper, seeded
4–5 spring onions (scallions)
60–75ml/4–5 tbsp olive oil
juice of 1 lemon
a small bunch of flat leaf parsley
1–2 cloves garlic, crushed
10–15ml/2–3 tsp ground sumac
salt and ground black pepper

1 First, prepare the flat bread. Toast it briefly on both sides, then break it into bitesize pieces. Set aside.

2 Chop the lettuce leaves, seed and chop the tomatoes, slice the carrot and radishes, chop the pepper, and slice the spring onions. Place all the vegetables in a bowl.

3 In a small bowl, whisk the olive oil with the lemon juice and garlic.

4 Add the chopped parsley to the vegetables, together with the toasted pieces of bread, then pour the dressing over the salad. Sprinkle the sumac over the top and season with salt and pepper. Toss the salad well, making sure the bread is well coated in the oil and sumac. Serve immediately as a side salad, as part of a meze spread, or on its own, in larger portions, as a snack or light lunch.

Nutritional information per portion: Energy 120kcal/499kJ; Protein 2.4g; Carbohydrate 7.7g, of which sugars 7.5g; Fat 9.1g, of which saturates 1.4g; Cholesterol 0mg; Calcium 54mg; Fibre 3g; Sodium 18mg.

Simple rice salad

In this quick and easy side dish, rice and a selection of chopped salad vegetables are served in a well-flavoured dressing to make a pretty salad.

SERVES 6

275g/10oz/1½ cups long grain rice

1 bunch spring onions (scallions), finely sliced

1 green (bell) pepper, seeded and finely diced

1 yellow (bell) pepper, seeded and finely diced

225g/8oz tomatoes, peeled, seeded and chopped

30ml/2 tbsp chopped fresh flat leaf parsley or coriander (cilantro)

FOR THE DRESSING

75ml/5 tbsp mixed olive oil and extra virgin olive oil

15ml/1 tbsp sherry vinegar

5ml/1 tsp strong Dijon mustard

salt and ground black pepper

1 Cook the rice in a large pan of lightly salted boiling water for 10–12 minutes, until tender but still al dente. Be careful not to overcook it.

2 Drain the rice well in a sieve (strainer), rinse thoroughly under cold running water and drain again. Leave the rice to cool completely.

3 Place the rice in a large serving bowl. Add the spring onions, peppers, tomatoes and parsley or coriander.

4 Make the dressing. Place all the ingredients in a screw-top jar, put the lid on and shake vigorously until well mixed. Stir the dressing into the rice and check the seasoning. Serve immediately.

Nutritional information per portion: Energy 280kcal/1166kJ; Protein 4.9g; Carbohydrate 42.3g, of which sugars 5.5g; Fat 10g, of which saturates 1.4g; Cholesterol 0mg; Calcium 40mg; Fibre 2g; Sodium 34mg.

Cracked wheat salad

Fresh herbs, bursting with the flavours of summer, are essential for this salad. Dried herbs will not make a suitable substitute.

SERVES 4

225 g/8 oz/1¹/₃ cups cracked wheat

350 ml/12 fl oz/1¹/₂ cups vegetable stock

1 cinnamon stick

pinch each of ground cumin, cayenne pepper and ground cloves

5ml/1 tsp salt

1 red and 1 yellow (bell) pepper, roasted

10 mangetouts, topped and tailed

2 tomatoes, peeled, seeded and diced

2 shallots, finely sliced

5 black olives, pitted and quartered

30ml/2 tbsp each shredded fresh basil, mint and parsley

30ml/2 tbsp roughly chopped walnuts

30ml/2 tbsp balsamic vinegar

120ml/4fl oz/¹/₂ cup virgin olive oil

ground black pepper

onion rings, to garnish

1 Place the cracked wheat in a large heatproof bowl. Pour the stock into a pan and bring to the boil with the spices and salt.

2 Cook for 1 minute, then pour the stock, with the cinnamon stick, over the cracked wheat. Leave to stand for 30 minutes.

3 Skin, seed and dice the peppers. In another bowl, mix together the peppers, mangetouts, tomatoes, shallots, olives, herbs and walnuts. Add the vinegar, olive oil and a little black pepper and stir thoroughly to mix.

4 Drain the cracked wheat of any liquid and discard the cinnamon stick. Place the cracked wheat in a serving bowl, stir in the fresh vegetable mixture and serve, garnished with onion rings.

Nutritional information per portion: Energy 223kcal/939kJ; Protein 6.9g; Carbohydrate 48.1g, of which sugars 15.9g; Fat 1.5g, of which saturates 0.2g; Cholesterol 0mg; Calcium 61mg; Fibre 2.9g; Sodium 35mg.

Parsley salad with bulgur wheat

This classic Lebanese salad, known as tabbouleh, is parsley, flavoured with a hint of mint and tossed with a little fine bulgur wheat so that the grains resemble tiny gems in a sea of green. Slice the parsley finely, rather than chop it, so that the strands remain dry and fresh, not mushy.

SERVES 4–6

65g/2¹⁄₂oz/¹⁄₂ cup fine bulgur wheat

juice of 2 lemons

a large bunch of flat leaf parsley (about 225g/8oz)

a handful of fresh mint leaves

2–3 tomatoes, skinned, seeded and finely diced

4 spring onions (scallions), trimmed and finely sliced

60ml/4 tbsp olive oil

salt and ground black pepper

1 cos or romaine lettuce, leaves separated, to serve

1 Rinse the bulgur wheat in cold water and drain well. Place it in a bowl and pour over the lemon juice. Leave to soften for 10 minutes while you prepare the salad.

2 With the parsley tightly bunched, slice the leaves as finely as you can with a sharp knife. Transfer the parsley to a bowl. Slice the mint leaves and add them to the bowl with the tomatoes, spring onions and the soaked bulgur wheat. Pour in the oil, season with salt and pepper and toss the salad gently.

3 Serve immediately, so that the herbs do not get the chance to soften. Arrange the lettuce leaves around the salad and use them to scoop up the tabbouleh.

Nutritional information per portion: Energy 232kcal/965kJ; Protein 5.2g; Carbohydrate 34.6g, of which sugars 2.7g; Fat 8.4g, of which saturates 1.1g; Cholesterol 0mg; Calcium 51mg; Fibre 1.4g; Sodium 12mg

Chickpea and bulgur wheat salad with mint

This is a traditional village salad, in which the ingredients are simply bound with olive oil and lemon juice and tossed with lots of fresh mint. The mixture can also be used as a filling for stuffed vine leaves or peppers and aubergines as an alternative to meat.

SERVES 4–6

150g/5oz/scant 1 cup fine bulgur
  wheat, rinsed
400g/14oz canned chickpeas, drained
  and rinsed
1 red onion, finely chopped
15–30ml/1–2 tbsp toasted sesame seeds
2–3 cloves garlic, crushed
60–75ml/4–5 tbsp olive oil
juice of 1–2 lemons
a bunch of flat leaf parsley, finely chopped
a large bunch of mint, coarsely chopped
salt and ground black pepper
5ml/1 tsp paprika, to garnish

1 Place the bulgur wheat in a heatproof bowl and pour over boiling water to cover. Leave to soak for 10–15 minutes, until it has doubled in volume.

2 Meanwhile, place the chickpeas in a bowl with the onion, sesame seeds and garlic and bind with the olive oil and lemon juice.

3 Squeeze the bulgur to remove any excess water and add it to the chickpeas with the parsley and mint. Toss well, season with salt and pepper to taste, and sprinkle the paprika over the top.

Nutritional information per portion: Energy 267kcal/1116kJ; Protein 8.6g; Carbohydrate 34.1g, of which sugars 3.3g; Fat 11.4g, of which saturates 1.4g; Cholesterol 0mg; Calcium 89mg; Fibre 4.1g; Sodium 153mg.

Fruity Salads

There is nothing so refreshing as a light fruit salad at the end of a meal, and there are so many varieties of fruit to choose from. Fragrant Fruit Salad, packed with exotic fruit, would be a fitting end to a dinner party, while Pistachio and Rose Water Oranges are an appropriate finale to a Middle Eastern repast. Zingy Papaya, Lime and Ginger Salad is perfect to get you off to a good start in the morning.

Fresh fig, apple and date salad

The contrasting textures of sweet Mediterranean figs and dates and crisp dessert apples combine especially well in this delicious salad.

SERVES 4

6 large eating apples
juice of ¹/₂ lemon
175g/6oz/generous 1 cup fresh dates
25g/1oz white marzipan
5ml/1 tsp orange flower water
60ml/4 tbsp natural (plain) yogurt
4 ripe green or purple figs
4 almonds, toasted

1 Core the apples. Slice thinly, then cut into fine matchsticks. Moisten with lemon juice to keep them white. Remove the stones (pits) from the dates and cut the flesh into fine strips, then combine them with the apple slices.

2 Soften the marzipan with the orange flower water and combine with the yogurt. Mix well.

3 Pile the apples and dates in the centre of four individual plates. Remove the stem from each of the figs and divide the fruit into quarters without cutting right through the base. Squeeze the base with the thumb and forefinger of each hand to open up the fig.

4 Place a fig in the centre of each fruit salad, spoon in the yogurt filling and decorate with a toasted almond.

Nutritional information per portion: Energy 223kcal/943kJ; Protein 4.5g; Carbohydrate 43.8g, of which sugars 43.7g; Fat 4.5g, of which saturates 0.4g; Cholesterol 0mg; Calcium 170mg; Fibre 4.8g; Sodium 46mg.

Fruit platter with spices

A simple fresh fruit platter sprinkled with spices makes a healthy dessert. It is low in fat and offers a range of essential vitamins and minerals as well as tasting wonderful.

SERVES 6

1 pineapple
2 papayas
1 small melon
juice of 2 limes
2 pomegranates
ground ginger and freshly grated nutmeg,
    for sprinkling
mint sprigs, to decorate

1 Peel the pineapple. Remove the core and any remaining eyes, then cut the flesh lengthways into thin wedges.

2 Peel the papayas, cut them in half, then cut into thin wedges. Halve the melon and remove the seeds. Cut into thin wedges and remove the skin.

3 Arrange the fruit on six individual plates and sprinkle with the lime juice.

4 Cut the pomegranates in half using a sharp knife, then scoop out the seeds, discarding any pith. Sprinkle the seeds over the fruit on the plates, then sprinkle the salad with a little ginger and nutmeg to taste. Decorate with sprigs of fresh mint and serve immediately.

Nutritional information per portion: Energy 55kcal/229kJ; Protein 1g; Carbohydrate 12.9g, of which sugars 12.9g Fat 0.3g, of which saturates 0g; Cholesterol 0g; Fibre 2.3g; Calcium 25mg; Sodium 0g.

Figs and pears in honey

This stunningly simple dessert of fresh figs and pears is scented with the warm fragrances of cinnamon and cardamom and drenched in a lemon and honey syrup.

SERVES 4

1 lemon
90ml/6 tbsp clear honey
1 cinnamon stick
1 cardamom pod
350ml/12fl oz/1/2 cups water
2 pears
8 fresh figs, halved

1 Pare the rind from the lemon using a cannelle knife (zester). Alternatively, use a vegetable peeler to remove the rind. Cut the pared rind into very thin strips.

2 Place the lemon rind, honey, cinnamon stick, cardamom pod and the water in a heavy pan and boil, uncovered, for about 10 minutes until reduced by about half.

3 Cut the pears into eighths, discarding the cores. Place in the syrup, add the figs and simmer for about 5 minutes, or until the fruit is tender.

4 Transfer the fruit to a serving bowl. Continue cooking the liquid until syrupy, then discard the cinnamon stick and cardamom pod and pour over the figs and pears to serve.

Nutritional information per portion: Energy 143kcal/606kJ; Protein 1.7g; Carbohydrate 34.4g, of which sugars 34.4g; Fat 0.7g, of which saturates 0g; Cholesterol 0mg; Calcium 109mg; Fibre 4.7g; Sodium 28mg.

Mixed melon salad with wild strawberries

Ice-cold melon is a delicious way to end a meal. Here several varieties are mixed with wild or woodland strawberries. If wild berries are not available, use ordinary strawberries or raspberries.

SERVES 4

1 cantaloupe or Charentais melon
1 Galia melon
900g/2lb watermelon
175g/6oz/1½ cups wild strawberries
4 fresh mint sprigs, to decorate

1 Halve all the melons using a large knife.

2 Remove the seeds from the cantaloupe and Galia melons with a spoon.

3 With a melon scoop, take out as many balls as you can from all three melons. Combine in a large bowl and chill.

4 Add the wild strawberries and turn out into four stemmed glass dishes.

5 Decorate with sprigs of fresh mint and serve.

Nutritional information per portion: Energy 204kcal/867kJ; Protein 3.9g; Carbohydrate 47.5g, of which sugars 47.5g; Fat 1.2g, of which saturates 0.3g; Cholesterol 0mg; Calcium 66mg; Fibre 2.9g; Sodium 128mg.

Refreshing fruit salad in a tangy dressing

In Indonesia, this salad often appears as a snack, as a salad to accompany fried and grilled dishes, or as a festive dish. Designed to be flexible, this refreshing salad, tossed in a pungent and tangy dressing, can include any choice of fruit and vegetables that you like.

SERVES 4–6

1 green mango, finely sliced
1 ripe, firm papaya, finely sliced
1–2 star fruit (carambola), finely sliced
1/2 pineapple, finely sliced and cut into
    bitesize pieces
1/2 pomelo, segmented
1 small cucumber, roughly peeled, seeded,
    and finely sliced
1 yam bean, finely sliced
a handful of beansprouts

FOR THE SAUCE

10ml/2 tsp terasi (shrimp paste)
225g/8oz roasted peanuts
4 garlic cloves, chopped
2–4 red chillies, seeded and chopped
15ml/1 tbsp tamarind paste
30ml/2 tbsp palm sugar (jaggery) or light
    muscavado (brown) sugar
salt

1 To make the sauce, dry-roast the terasi in a small, heavy frying pan until browned and emitting a toasted, pungent aroma.

2 Using a mortar and pestle or an electric blender, reduce the peanuts, garlic and chillies to a coarse paste. Beat in the dry-fried terasi, tamarind paste and sugar. Add enough water to make a thick, pouring sauce then stir until the sugar has dissolved. Season the sauce with salt to taste.

3 Put all the fruit and vegetables, except the beansprouts, into a large bowl. Pour in some of the sauce and toss gently together. Leave the salad to stand for 30 minutes.

4 Turn the salad into a serving dish. Sprinkle the beansprouts over the top and serve with the remaining sauce drizzled on top.

Nutritional information per portion: Energy 321kcal/1344kJ; Protein 12.3g; Carbohydrate 30g, of which sugars 27.2g; Fat 17.7g, of which saturates 3.3g; Cholesterol 8mg; Calcium 91mg; Fibre 6.2g; Sodium 81mg.

Cantaloupe melon with grilled strawberries

If strawberries are slightly underripe, sprinkling them with a little sugar and grilling them will help to bring out their flavour.

SERVES 4

115g/4oz/1 cup strawberries
15ml/1 tbsp icing (confectioners') sugar
½ cantaloupe melon

1 Preheat the grill (broiler) to high. Hull the strawberries and cut them in half.

2 Arrange the fruit in a single layer, cut side up, on a baking sheet or in an ovenproof dish and dust with the icing sugar.

3 Grill (broil) the strawberries for 4–5 minutes, or until the sugar starts to bubble and turn golden.

4 Meanwhile, scoop out the seeds from the half melon using a spoon. Using a sharp knife, remove the skin, then cut the flesh into wedges and arrange on a serving plate with the grilled strawberries. Serve immediately.

VARIATION
Use fragrant, orange-fleshed Charentais instead of cantaloupe.

Nutritional information per portion: Energy 53kcal/223kJ; Protein 0.9g; Carbohydrate 12.7g, of which sugars 12.7g; Fat 0.2g, of which saturates 0g; Cholesterol 0mg; Calcium 23mg; Fibre 0.8g; Sodium 41mg.

Melon trio with ginger cookies

The eye-catching colours of these three different melons really make this dessert, while the crisp biscuits provide a perfect textural contrast.

SERVES 4

¹/₄ watermelon
¹/₂ honeydew melon
¹/₂ Charentais melon
60ml/4 tbsp stem ginger syrup

FOR THE COOKIES

25g/1oz/2 tbsp unsalted butter
25g/1oz/2 tbsp caster (superfine) sugar
5ml/1 tsp clear honey
25g/1oz/¹/₄ cup plain (all-purpose) flour
25g/1oz/¹/₄ cup luxury glacé mixed fruit, finely chopped
1.5cm/¹/₂in piece of preserved stem ginger in syrup, drained and finely chopped
30ml/2 tbsp flaked (sliced) almonds

1 Remove the seeds from the melons, then cut them into wedges and slice off the rind. Cut into chunks and mix in a bowl. Add the stem ginger syrup, cover and chill.

2 Meanwhile, make the cookies. Preheat the oven to 180°C/350°F/ Gas 4. Place the butter, sugar and honey in a pan and heat until melted. Remove from the heat and stir in the remaining ingredients.

3 Line a baking sheet with baking parchment. Using half the mixture, place four spoonfuls on the paper,

leaving room to allow for spreading. Flatten the mixture slightly into rounds and bake for 15 minutes or until the tops are golden.

4 Leave to cool on the baking sheet for 1 minute, then lift each one in turn, using a metal spatula, and drape over a rolling pin to cool and harden. Repeat with the remaining mixture to make eight curved cookies.

5 Transfer the melon chunks and syrup to a serving dish or individual glasses and serve accompanied by the crisp ginger cookies.

Nutritional information per portion: Energy 350kcal/1479kJ; Protein 4.8g; Carbohydrate 65g, of which sugars 60.1g; Fat 9.7g, of which saturates 3.8g; Cholesterol 13mg; Calcium 74mg; Fibre 2.5g; Sodium 167mg.

Melon and strawberry salad

A beautiful and colourful fruit salad, with the flavour and fragrance of mint, this is equally suitable to serve as a refreshing appetizer or to round off a meal.

SERVES 4

1 Galia melon
1 honeydew melon
¹/₂ watermelon
225g/8oz/2 cups strawberries
15ml/1 tbsp lemon juice
15ml/1 tbsp clear honey
15ml/1 tbsp chopped fresh mint
1 fresh mint sprig (optional)

1 Prepare the melons by cutting them in half and discarding the seeds. Use a melon baller to scoop out the flesh into balls or alternatively a knife to cut it into cubes. Place these in a fruit bowl.

2 Rinse and hull the strawberries, cut in half and add to the melon balls or cubes.

3 Mix together the lemon juice and honey and add 15ml/1 tbsp water to make it easier to spoon over the fruit. Mix into the fruit gently.

4 Sprinkle the chopped mint over the top of the fruit. Serve the fruit salad decorated with the mint sprig, if wished.

Nutritional information per portion: Energy 204kcal/867kJ; Protein 3.9g; Carbohydrate 47.5g, of which sugars 47.5g; Fat 1.2g, of which saturates 0.3g; Cholesterol 0mg; Calcium 66mg; Fibre 2.9g; Sodium 128mg.

Fragrant fruit salad

Made from a medley of colourful and exotic fruit, this attractive, fresh-tasting salad is the perfect dessert for a dinner party.

SERVES 6

130g/4¹/₂oz/scant ³/₄ cup sugar
thinly pared rind and juice of 1 lime
150ml/¹/₄ pint/²/₃ cup water
60ml/4 tbsp brandy
5ml/1 tsp instant coffee granules or
    powder dissolved in 30ml/2 tbsp
    boiling water
1 small pineapple
1 papaya
2 pomegranates
1 mango
2 passion fruit or kiwi fruit
strips of lime rind, to decorate

1 Put the sugar and lime rind in a small pan with the water. Heat gently until the sugar dissolves, then bring to the boil and simmer for 5 minutes. Leave to cool, then strain into a large serving bowl, discarding the lime rind. Stir in the lime juice, brandy and dissolved coffee.

2 Using a sharp knife, cut the plume and stalk ends from the pineapple. Cut off the peel, then remove the central core and discard. Slice the flesh into bitesize pieces and add to the bowl.

3 Halve the papaya and scoop out the seeds. Cut away the skin, then slice the papaya. Halve the pomegranates and scoop out the seeds. Add to the bowl.

4 Cut the mango lengthways into three pieces, along each side of the stone (pit). Peel off the skin. Cut into chunks and add to the bowl.

5 Halve the passion fruit and scoop out the flesh, or peel and chop the kiwi fruit. Add to the bowl and serve, decorated with lime rind.

Nutritional information per portion: Energy 146kcal/620kJ; Protein 1g; Carbohydrate 33.2g, of which sugars 33.2g; Fat 0.3g, of which saturates 0g; Cholesterol 0mg; Calcium 40mg; Fibre 2.9g; Sodium 7mg.

Muscat grape frappé

This simple grape salad is worth making; the flavour and perfume of the Muscat grape is rarely more enticing than when captured in this sophisticated, icy-cool dish. Because of its alcohol content this dish is not suitable to serve to young children.

SERVES 4

½ bottle Muscat wine, Beaumes de
   Venise, Frontignan or Rivesaltes
450g/1lb Muscat grapes

1 Pour the wine into a stainless-steel or enamel tray, add 150ml/¼ pint/⅔ cup water and freeze for 3 hours, or until completely solid.

2 Remove the seeds from the grapes with a pair of tweezers.

3 If you have time, you can also remove the skin from the grapes. Scrape across the frozen wine with a tablespoon to make a fine ice.

4 Combine the grapes with the ice, spoon into four glasses and serve.

Nutritional information per portion: Energy 150kcal/634kJ; Protein 0.6g; Carbohydrate 22.5g, of which sugars 22.5g; Fat 0.1g, of which saturates 0g; Cholesterol 0mg; Calcium 27mg; Fibre 0.8g; Sodium 14mg.

Pistachio and rose water oranges

This light and tangy dessert is perfect to serve after a heavy main course, such as a hearty meat stew or a leg of roast lamb. Combining three favourite Middle-Eastern ingredients, it is delightfully fragrant and refreshing. If you don't have pistachio nuts, use hazelnuts instead.

SERVES 4

4 large oranges
30ml/2 tbsp rose water
30ml/2 tbsp shelled pistachio nuts,
   roughly chopped

1 Slice the top and bottom off one of the oranges. Using a serrated knife, slice down between the pith and the flesh, working round the orange, to remove the peel and pith.

2 Slice the orange into six rounds, reserving any juice. Repeat with the remaining oranges.

3 Arrange the oranges in a shallow dish. Mix the reserved juice with the rose water and drizzle over the orange slices.

4 Cover the dish with clear film (plastic wrap) and chill for about 30 minutes. Sprinkle the pistachio nuts over the oranges and serve.

Nutritional information per portion: Energy 101kcal/424kJ; Protein 3g; Carbohydrate 13.4g, of which sugars 13.2g; Fat 4.3g, of which saturates 0.6g; Cholesterol 0mg; Calcium 79mg; Fibre 3g; Sodium 47mg.

Fresh fruit salad

A light and refreshing fruit salad makes a healthy and nutritious end to a meal. The natural fruit sugars are kinder to the body than refined sugars.

SERVES 6

2 peaches
2 oranges
2 eating apples
16–20 strawberries
30ml/2 tbsp lemon juice
15–30ml/1–2 tbsp orange flower water
a few fresh mint leaves, to decorate

1 Place the peaches in a heatproof bowl and pour over boiling water. Leave to stand for 1 minute, then lift out with a slotted spoon, peel, stone (pit) and cut the flesh into thick slices.

2 Peel the oranges with a sharp knife, removing all the white pith, and segment them, catching any juice in a bowl.

3 Peel and core the apples and cut into thin slices. Using the point of a knife, hull the strawberries and halve or quarter the fruits if they are large. Place the prepared fruit in a large dish.

4 Blend together the lemon juice, orange flower water and any reserved orange juice. Pour the mixture over the salad and toss lightly. Serve decorated with a few fresh mint leaves.

Nutritional information per portion: Energy 29kcal/163kJ; Protein 0.8g; Carbohydrate 9.3g, of which sugars 9.3g; Fat 0.1g, of which saturates 0g; Cholesterol 0g; Fibre 1.6g; Calcium 10mg; Sodium 0mg.

Dressed strawberries

Fragrant strawberries release their finest flavour when moistened with a sauce of fresh raspberries and scented passion fruit.

SERVES 4

350g/12oz/2 cups raspberries, fresh or frozen
45ml/3 tbsp caster (superfine) sugar
1 passion fruit
675g/1¹/₂lb/6 cups small strawberries
8 plain finger biscuits (cookies), to serve

1 Place the raspberries and sugar in a stain-resistant pan and soften over a gentle heat to release the juices. Simmer for 5 minutes. Allow to cool.

2 Halve the passion fruit and scoop out the seeds and juice.

3 Turn the raspberries into a food processor or blender, add the passion fruit and blend until smooth.

4 Pass the blended fruit sauce through a fine nylon sieve (strainer) to remove the seeds.

5 Fold the strawberries into the sauce, then spoon into four stemmed glasses. Serve with plain finger biscuits.

Nutritional information per portion: Energy 113kcal/481kJ; Protein 2.7g; Carbohydrate 26.1g, of which sugars 26.1g; Fat 0.5g, of which saturates 0.1g; Cholesterol 0mg; Calcium 55mg; Fibre 4.2g; Sodium 14mg.

Zingy papaya, lime and ginger salad

This refreshing, fruity salad makes a lovely light breakfast, perfect for the summer months. Choose really ripe, fragrant papayas for the best flavour.

SERVES 4

2 large ripe papayas
juice of 1 fresh lime
2 pieces preserved stem ginger,
  finely sliced

1 Cut the papayas in half lengthways and scoop out the seeds, using a teaspoon. Using a sharp knife, cut the flesh into thin slices and arrange on a platter.

2 Squeeze the lime juice over the papayas and sprinkle with the sliced stem ginger. Serve immediately.

COOK'S TIP
Ripe papayas have a yellowish skin and feel soft to the touch. Their orange-coloured flesh has an attractive, smooth texture.

Nutritional information per portion: Energy 55kcal/233kJ; Protein 0.8g; Carbohydrate 13.4g, of which sugars 13.4g; Fat 0.2g, of which saturates 0g; Cholesterol 0mg; Calcium 35mg; Fibre 3.3g; Sodium 8mg.

Tropical scented fruit salad

With its special colour and exotic flavour, this fresh fruit salad is perfect after a rich meal. Serve the fruit salad with whipping cream flavoured with finely chopped drained preserved stem ginger.

SERVES 4–6

6 oranges
350–400g/12–14oz/3–3¹/₂ cups strawberries, hulled and halved
1–2 passion fruit
120ml/4fl oz/¹/₂ cup medium dry or sweet white wine

1 To segment the oranges, cut a slice off the top and bottom of each orange to expose the flesh. Place on a board and remove the skin, cutting downwards. Take care to remove all the white pith. Cut between the membranes to release the segments.

2 Put the orange segments in a serving bowl with the hulled and halved strawberries. Halve the passion fruit and, using a teaspoon, scoop the flesh into the bowl.

3 Pour the wine over the fruit and toss gently. Cover and chill in the refrigerator until ready to serve.

VARIATION
Use three small blood oranges and three ordinary oranges.

Nutritional information per portion: Energy 81kcal/342kJ; Protein 2g; Carbohydrate 15.6g, of which sugars 15.6g; Fat 0.2g, of which saturates 0g; Cholesterol 0mg; Calcium 75mg; Fibre 3g; Sodium 13mg.

Exotic fruit salad

Passion fruit makes a superb dressing for any fruit, but really brings out the flavour of exotic varieties. You can easily double the recipe, then serve the rest for the next day's breakfast.

SERVES 6

1 mango
1 papaya
2 kiwi fruit
coconut or vanilla ice cream, to serve

FOR THE DRESSING

3 passion fruit
thinly pared rind and juice of 1 lime
5ml/1 tsp hazelnut or walnut oil
15ml/1 tbsp clear honey

1 Peel the mango, cut it into three slices, then cut the flesh into chunks and place it in a large bowl. Peel the papaya and cut it in half. Scoop out the seeds, then chop the flesh.

2 Cut both ends off each kiwi fruit, then stand them on a board. Using a small sharp knife, cut off the skin from top to bottom. Cut each kiwi fruit in half lengthways, then cut into thick slices. Combine all the fruit in a large serving bowl.

3 To make the dressing, cut each passion fruit in half and scoop the seeds out into a sieve (strainer) set over a small bowl. Press well to extract all the juices. Lightly whisk the remaining dressing ingredients into the passion fruit juice, then pour the dressing over the prepared fruit in the serving bowl.

4 Mix gently to combine. Leave to chill for 1 hour before serving with scoops of coconut or vanilla ice cream.

Nutritional information per portion: Energy 66kcal/278kJ; Protein 1g; Carbohydrate 14.6g, of which sugars 14.5g; Fat 0.8g, of which saturates 0.1g; Cholesterol 0mg; Calcium 26mg; Fibre 2.9g; Sodium 7mg.

Fresh fruit with mango sauce

Fruit coulis became popular in the 1970s with nouvelle cuisine. It makes a simple fruit dish special and it is delicious with yogurt or ice cream.

SERVES 6

1 large ripe mango, peeled, stoned
   (pitted) and chopped
grated rind of 1 orange
juice of 3 oranges
caster (superfine) sugar, to taste
2 peaches
2 nectarines
1 small mango, peeled
2 plums
1 pear or ¹/₂ small melon
25–50g/1–2oz/2 heaped tbsp wild
   strawberries (optional)
25–50g/1–2oz/2 heaped tbsp raspberries
25–50g/1–2oz/2 heaped tbsp blueberries
juice of 1 lemon
small mint sprigs, to decorate

1 In a food processor fitted with the metal blade, process the large mango until smooth. Add the orange rind, juice and sugar to taste and process again until very smooth. Press through a sieve (strainer) into a bowl and chill the sauce.

2 Peel the peaches, if you like, then slice and stone (pit) the peaches, nectarines, small mango and plums. Quarter and core the pear, or if using, slice the melon thinly and remove the peel.

3 Place the sliced fruits on a large plate, sprinkle the fruits with the lemon juice and chill, covered with clear film (plastic wrap), for up to 3 hours before serving.

4 To serve, arrange the sliced fruits on serving plates, spoon the berries on top, drizzle with a little mango sauce and decorate with mint sprigs. Serve the remaining sauce separately.

Nutritional information per portion: Energy 82kcal/351kJ; Protein 1.9g; Carbohydrate 19.2g, of which sugars 19.1g; Fat 0.3g, of which saturates 0.1g; Cholesterol 0mg; Calcium 22mg; Fibre 3.3g; Sodium 5mg.

Dried fruit salad

This wonderful combination of fresh and dried fruit makes an excellent dessert throughout the year. Use frozen raspberries and blackberries during the winter months.

SERVES 4

115g/4oz/½ cup dried apricots
115g/4oz/½ cup dried peaches
1 pear
1 apple
1 orange
115g/4oz/⅔ cup mixed raspberries
   and blackberries
1 cinnamon stick
50g/2oz/¼ cup caster (superfine) sugar
15ml/1 tbsp clear honey
15ml/1 tbsp lemon juice

1 Soak the dried apricots and peaches in water for 1–2 hours, until plump, then drain and halve or quarter. Peel and core the pear and apple and cut into cubes.

2 Peel the orange with a sharp knife, removing all the pith, and cut into wedges. Place all the fruit in a large pan with the raspberries and blackberries.

3 Add 600ml/1 pint/2½ cups water, the cinnamon stick, sugar and honey and bring to the boil. Cover and simmer very gently for 10–12 minutes, then remove the pan from the heat.

4 Stir in the lemon juice. Allow to cool, then transfer to a bowl and chill in the refrigerator for 1–2 hours before serving.

Nutritional information per portion: Energy 162kcal/689kJ; Protein 3.1g; Carbohydrate 38.6g, of which sugars 38.6g; Fat 0.5g, of which saturates 0g; Cholesterol 0mg; Calcium 70mg; Fibre 5.9g; Sodium 13mg.

Dried fruit compote

Fruit compotes are a traditional Jewish dessert as they are light, healthy and refreshing after a heavy festive meal. Dried fruit compôtes are good in the winter when seasonal fruit is scarce.

SERVES 4

225g/8oz/1¹/₃ cups mixed dried fruit

75g/3oz/²/₃ cup dried cherries

75g/3oz/²/₃ cup sultanas (golden raisins)

10 prunes

10 dried apricots

hot, freshly brewed fragrant tea, such as
   Earl Grey or jasmine, to cover

15–30ml/1–2 tbsp sugar

¹/₄ lemon, sliced

60ml/4 tbsp brandy

1 Put the dried fruits in a bowl and pour over the hot tea. Add sugar to taste and the lemon slices. Cover with a plate, set aside and leave to cool to room temperature.

2 When the fruits have cooled sufficiently, chill in the refrigerator for at least 2 hours and preferably overnight. Just before serving, pour in the brandy and stir well.

Nutritional information per portion: Energy 189kcal/807kJ; Protein 2.6g; Carbohydrate 46.8g, of which sugars 46.8g; Fat 0.4g, of which saturates 0g; Cholesterol 0mg; Calcium 38mg; Fibre 5.3g; Sodium 20mg.

Salad Essentials

This guide includes information on the

main ingredients used in making

salads, from vegetables, salad leaves,

herbs and fruits to oils, vinegars,

dressings, dips and mayonnaises.

Useful facts are supplied on nutrition,

with practical advice on buying,

preparing and storing different foods.

Salad vegetables

Ingredients for making salads come in a huge range of shapes, colours, flavours and textures. Freshly picked and free from pesticides are best.

SHOOT VEGETABLES

This collection of vegetables, each with a distinctive flavour and appearance, ranges from aristocratic asparagus to the flowerbud-like globe artichoke.

Fennel

Florence fennel is related to the herb and spice of the same name. The short, fat bulbs have a similar texture to celery and are topped with edible feathery fronds. Fennel has a mild aniseed flavour, which is most potent when eaten raw. Cooking tempers and sweetens the flavour. When using fennel raw, slice it thinly or chop roughly, and add to salads. Or, cut into wedges and steam, or brush with olive oil and roast or cook on a griddle, then serve sprinkled with balsamic vinegar. Fennel is best when fresh and should be eaten as soon as possible.

Fennel is a diuretic and also has a calming and toning effect on the stomach. Low in calories, it contains beta carotene and folate. Fennel seeds are very good for the digestion.

LEFT: *Fennel*

Asparagus

There are two main types: white asparagus is picked just before it sprouts above the surface of the soil; green-tipped asparagus develops its colour when it comes into contact with sunlight, and is cut above the ground. It takes three years to grow a crop from seed. Before use, scrape the stalk's lower half with a vegetable peeler, then trim off the woody end. Briefly poach whole spears in a frying pan with a little boiling salted water, or tie the spears in a bundle and boil upright in an asparagus boiler or a tall asparagus pan. Cool slightly, then serve the asparagus with a lemony home-made mayonnaise or vinaigrette dressing.

Asparagus was used as a medicine long before it was eaten as a food. It is a rich source of vitamin C and has diuretic and laxative properties.

ABOVE: *Asparagus*

Chicory

This shoot has long, tightly packed leaves. There are two kinds: white and red. Red chicory has a stronger flavour, while the white variety has crisper leaves. The crisp texture and slightly bitter taste means that chicory is ideal for salads. Chicory can be steamed or braised, although in cooking, sadly, the red-leafed variety fades to brown. Before use, remove outer leaves and wash, then trim the base. In natural medicine, chicory is sometimes used to treat gout and rheumatism. It is a digestive and liver stimulant, and good for a spring tonic.

ABOVE: *Chicory*

Celery

Like asparagus, celery was once grown primarily for medicinal reasons. Serve raw to make a crunchy salad. Celery leaves have a tangy taste and can add flavour to stocks. Low in calories, but rich in vitamin C and potassium, celery is a recognized diuretic and sedative.

Globe artichokes

Once cooked, the purple-tinged leaves have an exquisite flavour. Eat them with the fingers, dipping each leaf into vinaigrette dressing, then draw each leaf through the teeth and eat the fleshy part. The heart is good sliced in to a salad. Globe artichokes are a source of fibre, vitamins A and C, iron, calcium and potassium.

VEGETABLE FRUITS

By cultivation and use, tomatoes, avocados and (bell) peppers are treated as vegetables, but botanically they are classified as fruit.

Tomatoes

There are dozens of varieties to choose from, which vary in colour, shape and size. The egg-shaped plum tomato, when fully ripe, is perfect for cooking because it has a rich flavour and a high proportion of flesh to seeds. Bought tomatoes can be bland and tasteless because they have been picked too young. Vine-ripened and cherry tomatoes are sweet and juicy and are good in salads or uncooked sauces. Large beefsteak tomatoes have a good flavour and are also excellent for salads. Vine-ripened tomatoes are higher in vitamin C than those picked when they are still green.

They are also a source of vitamin E, beta carotene, magnesium, calcium and phosphorus. Tomatoes contain the bioflavonoid lycopene, which is believed to prevent some forms of cancer. It is thought to work by reducing the harmful effects of free radicals.

ABOVE: *Tomatoes*

(Bell) Peppers

Like chillies, sweet peppers are members of the capsicum family. They range in colour from green through to orange, yellow, red and even purple. Green peppers are fully developed but not completely ripe. They have refreshing, juicy flesh with a crisp texture. Other colours of peppers are more mature, have sweeter flesh, and are more digestible than less ripe green peppers. They can be stuffed or sliced into salads.

BELOW: *(Bell) peppers*

Avocados

Although avocados have a high fat content, the fat is monounsaturated, and is thought to lower blood cholesterol levels in the body. Avocados also contain valuable amounts of vitamins C and E, iron, potassium and manganese. They are rich in flavour and add a good colour and texture to a salad. The flesh can be sliced or scooped out with a spoon, then sprinkled with lemon juice to prevent browning.

ABOVE: *Avocados*

ABOVE: *Cucumber*

Cucumbers

These are juicy and have a crisp texture and refreshing, cool taste. Varieties include English cucumbers, ridged cucumbers, gherkins and kirbys. They are used in many salads.

Garlic

When the thin skin is papery dry, the cloves are mature and will burst with flavour. Always look out for a firm head when buying garlic.

When crushed and added to a vinaigrette dressing with olive oil and mustard, it imparts an assertive flavour. If a milder taste is required, the salad bowl can be rubbed with a raw clove of garlic to add flavour. Garlic is said to impart health benefits, mainly to the heart.

BELOW: *Garlic*

Salad Leaves

It is only a few years since the most exotic lettuce available was the crisp-textured iceberg. Today, salad leaves come in a huge variety of shapes, sizes, colours and flavours, from bitter-tasting endive to peppery rocket (arugula) and red-leafed lollo rosso. Making a mixed leaf salad has never been so easy.

Salad leaves are best when they are very fresh and do not keep well. Avoid leaves that are wilted, discoloured or shrivelled. Store in the refrigerator, unwashed, for between 2 days and 1 week, depending on the variety. As salad leaves are routinely sprayed with pesticides, they should be washed thoroughly, but gently, to avoid damaging the leaves, and then dried with a dish towel. Better still, choose organically grown produce.

Although all types of salad

leaves are about 90 per cent water, they contain useful amounts of vitamins and minerals, particularly folate, iron and the antioxidants, vitamin C and beta carotene. The outer, darker leaves tend to be more nutritious than the paler leaves in the centre. More importantly, like other green, leafy vegetables, their antioxidant content has been found to guard against the risk of many cancers. Salad leaves are usually eaten raw when nutrients are at their strongest. Lettuce is reputed to have a calming effect.

Cultivated for thousands of years, lettuces were probably first eaten as a salad vegetable during Roman times. Nutritionally, lettuce is best eaten raw, but it can be braised, steamed or made into a soup. Large-

ABOVE: *Lamb's lettuce*

leafed varieties can be used to wrap around a filling.

Butterhead lettuce
This soft-leafed lettuce has an unassuming flavour and is good as a sandwich-filler.

Cos lettuce
Known since Roman times, the cos lettuce has long, sturdy leaves and a strong flavour. Little Gem (Bibb) is a baby version of cos and has firm, densely packed leaves.

Iceberg lettuce
This lettuce has a round, firm head of pale-green leaves with a crisp texture. Like the butterhead, it has a mild, slightly bitter flavour and is best used as a garnish. It is reputed to be one of the most highly chemically treated crops, so it is a good idea to choose organic iceberg lettuces if you can.

Oak leaf
This attractive lettuce has red-tinged, soft-textured leaves with a slightly bitter flavour. In salads, combine oak

LEFT: *Clockwise from left: curly endive, oak leaf, cos, butterhead and iceberg lettuces*

BELOW: *Radicchio*

used in a salad or as a base for roasted vegetables. Lollo biondo is a pale-green version.

Lamb's lettuce

This tiny lettuce has a cluster of small, rounded, velvety leaves with a delicate flavour. Serve lamb's lettuce on its own, or mix with other leaves and lettuces.

Curly endive

Also known as frisée, curly endive has spiky, ragged leaves that are dark green on the outside and fade to an attractive pale yellow-green toward its centre. It has a distinctive bitter flavour that can be enhanced by a robust dressing.

Radicchio

A member of the chicory family, radicchio has deep-red, tightly packed leaves that have a bitter peppery flavour. It is good in salads and can be sautéed or roasted.

Rocket (Arugula)

Classified as a herb, rocket is a popular addition to many salads, or it can be served as a starter with thin shavings of Parmesan cheese. It has a very distinctive, strong, peppery flavour, which is more robust when the rocket is wild. Lightly steamed rocket has a milder flavour than the raw leaves but it is still equally delicious.

Sorrel

The long pointed leaves of sorrel have a refreshing, sharp flavour that is best when mixed in a salad with milder tasting leaves. This salad leaf contains oxalic acid, which, when cooked, will inhibit the body's absorption of iron. Sorrel also acts as an effective diuretic.

Watercress

The hot, peppery flavour of watercress complements milder tasting salad leaves and is classically combined with sweet fresh orange. It does not keep well and is best used within two days of purchase. Watercress is a member of the cruciferous family and shares its cancer-fighting properties.

BELOW: *Rocket*

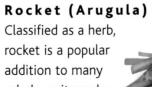

BELOW: *Sorrel*

BELOW: *Watercress*

leaf with a mixture of green lettuces for a wonderful contrast of tastes and textures.

Lollo rosso

The pretty, frilly leaves of lollo rosso are green at the base and a deep, autumn-red around the edge. Its imposing shape means that it is best mixed with other leaves if

Herbs

Herbs can make a significant difference to the flavour and aroma of a dish and they have the ability to enliven the simplest of salads.

Fresh herbs are widely available, sold loose, in packets or growing in pots. The packets do not keep for as long and should be stored in the refrigerator. Place stems of fresh herbs in a half-filled jar of water and cover with a plastic bag. Sealed with an elastic band, the herbs should keep in the refrigerator for a week. Growing herbs should be kept on a sunny windowsill. If watered regularly, and not cut too often, they will keep for months.

Basil

This delicate aromatic herb is widely used in Italian dishes and is added to tomato and mozzarella salad. The leaves bruise easily, so are best used whole or torn, rather than cut.

LEFT: *Basil*

Chives

A member of the onion family, chives have a milder flavour and are often used as a garnish or chopped over egg or potato salads, or added to green salads. Like onions, chives are an antiseptic and act as a digestive.

Coriander (Cilantro)

Warm and spicy, coriander is delicious in salads. It looks similar to flat leaf parsley but its taste is completely different. It is often sold with its root intact.Coriander is an effective digestive, easing indigestion and nausea.

ABOVE: *Dill*

Dill

The mild, yet distinctive, aniseed flavour of dill goes well with potatoes, courgettes (zucchini) and cucumber. It can be added to a wide variety of egg dishes, such as egg mayonnaise and is perfect in fish salads, or with marinated herring or gravadlax. It can be added to salad dressings and is a good partner for mustard. An attractive herb with delicate, wispy leaves, add to dishes just prior to serving as it tends to wilt quickly. Dill is a popular herb for settling the stomach and is thought to reduce flatulence.

Mint

The most familiar types are spearmint and peppermint, but there are other distinct-flavoured varieties, such as apple, lemon and pineapple mint, which make a refreshing drink when infused in boiling water. Mint is

ABOVE: *Coriander (cilantro)*

used as a flavouring in a wide variety of dishes, from stuffings to fruit salads. It is a traditional cure for nausea and indigestion, and is also stimulates and cleanses the system.

ABOVE: *Parsley*

Parsley

There are two types of parsley: flat leaf and curly. Both taste relatively similiar, and either will impart a delicious fresh taste when added to salads. Curly parsley is easier to chop very finely, while flat leaf parsley makes a pretty garnish. Parsley is an excellent source of vitamin C, iron and calcium. Chewing parsley after eating garlic or onions can neutralize the smell and freshen the breath.

Fruits

At the end of a meal, a refreshing fruit salad makes a good palate cleanser, and the possible variations of ingredients are many.

Mangoes

Rich in vitamin C and carotene, mangoes are reputed to cleanse the blood. For an exotic tropical fruit salad, cube mangoes, papayas, kiwi fruits and pineapple, and drizzle with freshly squeezed orange juice and a little maple syrup.

BELOW: *Mangoes*

Pineapples

Organic pineapples have a high enzyme content, one of which, bromelain, deeply cleanses the digestive system, aiding the uptake of all nutritional compounds. Pineapples contain high amounts of vitamin C and they are good for the complexion, especially when they are applied to the skin.

ABOVE: *Pineapple*

Dates

Organic dates are a rich source of dietary fibre, potassium and folic acid. Naturally sweet, they are great added chopped to fruit salads and steamed puddings, or you can just eat them whole. They are great energy boosters for athletes, pregnant women and the elderly. They can also be given to children instead of sweets (candies).

BELOW: *Dates*

Peaches

Peaches are sweet and tasty in fruit salads. They can help to regulate the system and ease constipation. Ripe peaches should be stored in the refrigerator but brought to room temperature before eating.

ABOVE: *Peaches*

Raspberries

These soft and fragrant berries are effective in removing toxins from the body. They can be added to any fruit salad with a little maple syrup to taste, and a splash of lemon juice to bring out the flavour. Store in the refrigerator for two days.

BELOW: *Strawberries*

Strawberries

Strawberries are naturally sweet and delicious. As with all berries and grapes, they are high in vitamin C.

BELOW: *Grapes*

Grapes

Naturally high in antioxidants. They provide the perfect pick-up for convalescents, being a good source of carbohydrates and vitamin C. Grapes are also easy to eat and taste delicious. Eat them at any time except after a big meal, as they tend to ferment and upset the stomach if it is full. They are best eaten straight off the bunch, or chopped into fruit salads, and taste excellent in fresh green salads.

BELOW: *Raspberries*

Oils

There are a wide variety of oils that can be used in salad dressings. They are produced from fruits, such as olives; from nuts, such as walnuts, almonds and hazelnuts; and from seeds, such as rapeseed, safflower and sunflower. Virgin oils, which are obtained from the first cold pressing, are sold unrefined, have the most characteristic flavour and they are the most expensive.

Olive oil

Indisputably the king of oils, olive oil varies in flavour and colour, depending on how it is made and where it comes from. Climate, soil, harvesting and pressing all influence the end result – generally, the hotter the climate, the more robust the oil. Thus oils from southern Italy, Greece and Spain have a stronger flavour and a darker colour than those from the rest of Italy and from France. Olive oil is rich in monounsaturated fat, which has been found to reduce cholesterol, thereby reducing the risk of heart disease. There are different grades to choose from, such as extra virgin olive oil which has a low acidity – less than 1 per cent. It is excellent in salad dressings. Virgin olive oil is also a pure first-pressed oil; this has a slightly higher level of acidity than extra virgin olive oil, and can be used in much the same way.

LEFT: *Extra virgin olive oil*

BELOW: *Groundnut (peanut) oil (left) and almond oil*

Other oils

There is a wide range of light, processed oils on the market that are all relatively taste-free and have a variety of uses in the kitchen, such as corn oil, safflower oil, sunflower oil, rapeseed (canola) oil and soya oil.

ABOVE: *Walnut, sesame and hazelnut oils*

Groundnut oil is also known as peanut oil, is relatively tasteless and useful for frying, cooking and dressings.

Speciality oils such as sesame oil, walnut oil, hazelnut oil and almond oil are richly flavoured and are therefore used in small quantities, often as a flavouring ingredient for salad dressings and marinades.

Essential Fats

We all need some fat in our diet. It keeps us warm, adds flavour to our food, carries essential vitamins A, D, E and K around the body, and provides essential fatty acids, which cannot be produced in the body, but are vital for growth and development, and may reduce the risk of heart attacks.

What is more important is the type and amount of fat that we eat. Some fats are better for us than others, and we should adjust our intake accordingly. It is recommended that fat should make up no more than 35 per cent of our diet.

Vinegars

One of our oldest condiments, vinegar is made by acetic fermentation, a process that occurs when a liquid with less than 18 per cent alcohol is exposed to the air.

Most countries produce their own type of vinegar, often based on their most popular alcoholic drink – wine in France and Italy; sherry in Spain; rice wine in Asia; beer and cider in Great Britain, and apple cider vinegar in the USA. It is a common ingredient in salad dressings.

Wine vinegars

These can be made from white, red or rosé wine. The quality of the vinegar depends on the original ingredient and the method of production. The finest wine vinegars are made by the

ABOVE: *Rice vinegar (left) and brown malt vinegar*

LEFT: *Balsamic vinegar*

BELOW: *Sherry vinegar*

Orleans method. Cheaper methods of fermentation involve heating, which produces a harsher vinegar. Use in dressings and mayonnaise.

Balsamic vinegar

Rich, dark and mellow, this vinegar originates from northern Italy. Made from grape juice (predominantly from Trebbiano grapes), it is fermented in vast wooden barrels for a minimum of four to five years and up to 40 or more years, resulting in a rich vinegar with a concentrated flavour.

Balsamic vinegar is delicious in salad dressings.

Sherry vinegar

This vinegar can be as costly as balsamic vinegar and, if left to mature in wooden barrels, can be equally good. Sweet and mellow, it is used in the same way as balsamic.

Malt vinegar

Made from soured beer, malt vinegar is used for pickling onions and other vegetables, or for sprinkling over chips (French fries). It can be clear, but is often sold coloured with caramel. Malt vinegar's robust, harsh flavour is not suitable for salad dressings.

Cider vinegar

Made from cider and praised for its health-giving properties, cider vinegar has a slight apple flavour, but is too strong and sharp to use in the same ways as wine vinegar. It can be used for salad dressings and is particularly good in mushroom salads.

Rice vinegar

There are two kinds of rice vinegar: the type from Japan is mellow and sweet, and often used to flavour sushi rice, but it can also be added to dressings; Chinese rice vinegar is a much sharper variety. Rice vinegar is usually a clear pale-brown colour.

BELOW AND RIGHT: *Red and white wine vinegars*

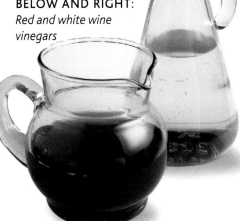

Salad Dressings

Although the ingredients of a salad are important, the secret of a perfect salad is a good dressing. A French dressing made from the best olive oil and vinegar can improve the dullest selection of lettuce leaves, while a home-made mayonnaise is impressive. The safest way of creating a perfect dressing is to prepare it in advance. Home-made dressings can be stored in the refrigerator for up to a week and will improve in flavour. Here is a selection of dressings that will enhance any salad.

Thousand island Dressing

This creamy dressing is great with green salads and grated carrot, hot potato, pasta and rice salads.

INGREDIENTS

Makes about 120ml/4fl oz/½ cup
60ml/4 tbsp sunflower oil
15ml/1 tbsp orange juice
15ml/1 tbsp lemon juice
10ml/2 tsp grated lemon rind
15ml/1 tbsp finely chopped onion
5ml/1 tsp paprika
5ml/1 tsp Worcestershire sauce
15ml/1 tbsp finely chopped fresh parsley
salt and ground black pepper

Put all the ingredients into a screw-top jar and season to taste. Replace the lid and shake well.

French Dressing

French vinaigrette is the most widely used salad dressing.

INGREDIENTS

Makes about 120ml/4fl oz/½ cup
90ml/6 tbsp extra virgin olive oil
15ml/1 tbsp white wine vinegar
5ml/1 tsp French mustard
pinch of caster (superfine) sugar

1 Place the oil and vinegar in a jar.

2 Add the mustard and sugar.

3 Replace the lid and shake well.

French Herb Dressing

The delicate scents and flavours of fresh herbs are perfect in a French dressing. Use just one herb or a selection. Toss with a green salad and serve with cheese, bread and wine.

INGREDIENTS

Makes about 120ml/4fl oz/½ cup
60ml/4 tbsp extra virgin olive oil
30ml/2 tbsp groundnut (peanut) or
    sunflower oil
15ml/1 tbsp lemon juice
60ml/4 tbsp finely chopped fresh herbs
    (parsley, chives, tarragon and marjoram)
pinch of caster (superfine) sugar

1 Place the olive oil and groundnut or sunflower oil in a screw-top jar.

2 Add the lemon juice, chopped fresh herbs and sugar.

3 Replace the lid and shake well.

Mayonnaise

Mayonnaise is a simple emulsion made with egg yolks and oil. For consistent results, ensure that both egg yolks and oil are at room temperature before combining. Home-made mayonnaise is made with raw egg yolks and may therefore be considered unsuitable for young children, pregnant mothers and the elderly.

INGREDIENTS

Makes about 300ml/¹/₂ pint/1¹/₄ cups
2 egg yolks
5ml/1 tsp French mustard
150ml/¹/₄ pint/²/₃ cup extra virgin
   olive oil
150ml/¹/₄ pint/²/₃ cup groundnut (peanut)
   or sunflower oil
10ml/2 tsp white wine vinegar
salt and ground black pepper

1 Place the egg yolks and mustard in a food processor and blend smoothly.
2 Add the olive oil a little at a time while the processor is running. When the mixture is thick, add the groundnut or sunflower oil in a slow, steady stream.
3 Add the vinegar and season the mayonnaise to taste with salt and ground black pepper.

Yogurt Dressing

This is a less rich version of a classic mayonnaise and is easier to make if you use ready-made mayonnaise. It can be used as a low-fat substitute and is a versatile salad dressing. You can vary the herbs according to taste.

INGREDIENTS

Makes about 210ml/7fl oz/scant 1 cup
150ml/¹/₄ pint/²/₃ cup plain (natural) yogurt
30ml/2 tbsp mayonnaise
30ml/2 tbsp milk
15ml/1 tbsp chopped fresh parsley
15ml/1 tbsp chopped fresh chives
salt and ground black pepper

Put all the ingredients together in a bowl. Season to taste and mix well.

Blue Cheese and Chive Dressing

Blue cheese dressings have a strong, robust flavour and are traditionally served with chicken wings or steak. However, they are also well suited to serving as a dip with crudités such as carrots and avocados, or with salad leaves such as escarole, lettuce, chicory and radicchio.

INGREDIENTS

Makes about 350ml/12fl oz/1¹/₂ cups
75g/3oz blue cheese (Stilton, Bleu
   d'Auvergne, Roquefort or Gorgonzola)
150ml/¹/₄ pint/²/₃ cup medium fat
   plain (natural) yogurt
45ml/3 tbsp olive oil
30ml/2 tbsp lemon juice
15ml/1 tbsp chopped fresh chives
ground black pepper

1 Remove the rind from the cheese and combine with a third of the yogurt in a bowl. Beat with a wooden spoon to mix thoroughly.

2 Add the remainder of the yogurt, the olive oil and the lemon juice. Mix well.

3 Stir in the chopped chives and season to taste with ground black pepper. Chill the dressing if not using it immediately, or serve at once with a selection of crudités.

Basil and Lemon Mayonnaise

This luxurious dressing is flavoured with lemon juice and two types of basil. Serve with all kinds of leafy salads, crudités or coleslaws. It is also good with baked potatoes, spicy potato wedges or as a delicious dip for chips (French fries). The dressing will keep in an airtight jar for up to a week in the refrigerator.

INGREDIENTS

Makes about 300ml/¹⁄₂ pint/1¹⁄₄ cups

2 large (US extra large) egg yolks

15ml/1 tbsp lemon juice

150ml/¹⁄₄ pint/²⁄₃ cup extra virgin
    olive oil

150ml/¹⁄₄ pint/²⁄₃ cup sunflower oil

4 garlic cloves

handful of fresh green basil

handful of fresh opal basil

salt and ground black pepper

1 Place the egg yolks and lemon juice in a blender or food processor and mix them briefly until lightly blended.

2 In a jug (pitcher), stir together the olive oil and sunflower oil. With the machine running, pour in the oil very slowly, a little at a time.

3 Once half of the oil has been added, and the dressing has successfully emulsified, the remaining oil can be incorporated more quickly. Continue processing until a thick, creamy mayonnaise has formed.

4 Peel and crush the garlic cloves and add to the mayonnaise. Alternatively, place the cloves on a chopping board and sprinkle with salt, then flatten them with the heel of a heavy-bladed knife and chop the flesh. Flatten the garlic again to make a coarse purée. Add to the mayonnaise.

BELOW: *Basil and lemon mayonnaise.*

5 Remove the basil stalks and tear both types of leaves into small pieces. Stir into the mayonnaise.

6 Add salt and pepper to taste, then transfer the mayonnaise to a serving dish. Cover and chill until ready to serve.

INSTANT DRESSINGS AND DIPS

If you need an instant dressing or dip, try one of these quick and easy recipes. Most of them use store-cupboard (pantry) ingredients.

Creamy black olive dip

Stir a little black olive paste into a carton of extra-thick double (heavy) cream until smooth and well blended. Add salt, ground black pepper and a squeeze of lemon juice to taste. Serve chilled.

Crème fraîche dressing with spring onions

Finely chop a bunch of spring onions (scallions) and stir into a carton of crème fraîche. Add a dash of chilli sauce, a squeeze of lime juice, and salt and ground black pepper.

Greek yogurt and mustard dip

Mix a small carton of Greek (US strained plain) yogurt with 5–10ml/ 1–2 tsp wholegrain mustard. Serve with crudités.

Herb mayonnaise

Liven up ready-made mayonnaise with a handful of chopped fresh herbs – try flat leaf parsley, basil, dill or tarragon.

Passata and horseradish dip

Bring a little tang to a small carton or bottle of passata (bottled strained tomatoes) by adding some horseradish sauce or 5–10ml/1–2 tsp

creamed horseradish and salt and pepper to taste. Serve the dip with crudités or lightly-cooked vegetables.

Pesto dip

For a simple, speedy, Italian-style dip, stir 15ml/1 tbsp ready-made red or green pesto into a carton of sour cream. Serve with crisp crudités or wedges of oven-roasted Mediterranean vegetables, such as (bell) peppers, courgettes (zucchini) and onions, for a delicious appetizer.

Soft cheese and chive dip

Mix a tub of soft cheese with 30–45ml/2–3 tbsp chopped fresh chives and season to taste with salt and black pepper. If the dip is too

ABOVE: *Top row: creamy black olive dip, crème fraîche dressing with spring onions. Second row: herb mayonnaise, sun-dried tomato dip. Third row: Greek yogurt and mustard dip, soft-cheese and chive dip, spiced yogurt dressing. Fourth row: pesto dip, passata and horseradish dip.*

thick, stir in a little milk to soften it. Use as a dressing for all kinds of salads, especially winter coleslaws.

Spiced yogurt dressing

Stir a little curry paste and chutney into a carton of yogurt.

Sun-dried tomato dip

Stir 15–30ml/1–2 tbsp sun-dried tomato paste into a carton of Greek (US strained plain) yogurt. Season to taste with salt and black pepper.

Index